THE GREAT FLORIDA CRAFT BEER GUIDE

SEASIDE PUBLISHING

Seaside Publishing
Gainesville
Tallahassee
Tampa
Boca Raton
Pensacola
Orlando
Miami
Jacksonville
Ft. Myers
Sarasota

The Great Florida Craft Beer Guide

Mark DeNote

Foreword by Joey Redner

Historic posters and advertisements are courtesy of Mike Zane. Swamp Head Brewery photo is courtesy of Stefanie Crockett. Funky Buddha photo is courtesy of George Mercado Photography. All other photos are by the author.

19 18 17 16 15 14   6 5 4 3 2 1

Printed in the United States of America on recycled, acid-free paper

Library of Congress Control Number: 2014937650
ISBN 978-0-942084-26-9

 Seaside Publishing is a division
of the University Press of Florida.

For a complete list of Seaside books, please contact us
Seaside Publishing
15 Northwest 15th Street
Gainesville, FL 32611-2079
1-352-392-6867
1-800-226-3822
orders@upf.com
www.seasidepublishing.com

This book is dedicated to the person
who stood by me and did not laugh
hysterically when I told her I wanted
to write a book about beer.
To my wife, my love, and my friend, Carrie.

PERMIT NO. FLA. U-500   CONTENTS 12 FL. OZ.

PILSNER STYLE BEER

Jax

EXTRA FINE

JAX BREWING CO. Jacksonville, Fla.

GUARANTEED 12% ORIGINAL EXTRACT

TAX PAID AT THE RATE PRESCRIBED BY INTERNAL REVENUE LAW

INTERNAL REVENUE TAX PAID CONTENTS 12 FLUID OUNCES

A
Ace High
Spearman

ENGLISH-TYPE
ALE

GUARANTEED NATURAL PRODUCT OF AN ALL GRAIN ALE BREW
FULLY TOP-FERMENTED WITH GENUINE IMPORTED ENGLISH ALE YEAST
THE SPEARMAN BREWING CO., PENSACOLA, FLORIDA

LUCKY 7%
ALE

GOLD TOP BREWING
CORPORATION
HIALEAH, FLA.

INTERNAL REVENUE
TAX PAID
CONTENTS 18 FL. OZ.

CONTENTS

FOREWORD

When I decided to open Cigar City Brewing a significant part of the motivation was a selfish one. There were the normal motivations one would expect a fledgling brewery owner to possess: a desire to make a living pursuing a passion, a deep confidence in the concept and the market, and ultimately the faith that my nascent brewery could find a home in the Tampa Bay area and Florida. There was certainly an ulterior motive, too: a motivation that had a lot to do with the Florida beer scene as I found it prior to opening Cigar City Brewing in 2009.

As a craft beer drinker, I simply craved more variety than the precious little to be found in the Florida beer scene throughout much of the first decade of the new millennium. I pined for a thriving beer scene with many growing and diversely style-focused breweries, each making beers that reflected their individual tastes and passions. A beer scene like I had encountered in so many other cities throughout my travels. It wasn't that there was no good Florida-brewed beer. There was good Florida beer to be had, without a doubt, but by and large locally produced beer was relegated to brewpubs, most of which were far from me, and things like freshly filled growlers or locally packaged beer on grocers' shelves were virtually nonexistent. There was little visible critical mass that suggested a thriving brewing scene would soon be on its way. This longing for a more diverse beer scene in the state I love ultimately pushed me over the tipping point and convinced me to make a really big gamble.

As a fifth-generation and lifelong Floridian and Tampa native, I naturally went through my "beer education" and had my first drinking experiences primarily in Florida but travel to other states and countries showed me a world of possibilities and could-be's. In my experience, the people in beer-centric cities like Portland, Brussels, Denver, and San Diego were not possessed of intrinsically different tastes than the people of Tampa. What brewery owners in those cities knew was that a significant percentage of the population everywhere will always yearn for new, unique, and even intense flavor experiences.

While Florida has arrived later to the craft beer game than other regions of the United States, it has made up for lost time. Today, breweries are proliferating like mushrooms after a warm Florida rain. As a brewery owner, I celebrate this new wave of Florida beer brewing "competitors." I remain optimistic that each will add positively to the local color and culture of Florida. Local breweries, unlike many other businesses, become deeply ingrained in the fabric of their communities and regions. The beers they produce often harbor deep associations for locals and visitors alike. Like a local food specialty or landmark, beer can take on a symbolism that goes far beyond just the tangible can, bottle, or keg. It is in these associations, in the emotional connections made by each of us, that true history lives. Beyond simple facts and dates lies the heart of history. What a person, place, or even a product means to the people of a region or to how a visitor experiences that place is the true stuff of history.

In his *Great Florida Craft Beer Guide*, Mark DeNote provides a regional history that for better or worse closely follows America's beer history through the locally produced and locally owned smaller breweries of the late 1800s, the dark times of prohibition, the dominance of mega-breweries and the decline of the community, neighborhood, and even regional breweries through the 1960s, and the long stasis-like period of consolidation and international acquisition. As brewery ownership changes hands, becoming increasing global, actual product variety decreases. Mark covers the first fumbling steps back toward hand-crafted and local, chronicling breweries that were part of the first Microbrew Boom and Bust of the early nineties and brings the story up to our latest, seemingly more sustainable renaissance from nano-breweries to true regional production.

Florida's beer-producing past is a much older and richer history than anyone would expect. In many ways, the history of beer in Florida is also the history of Florida's growth from an underpopulated backwater to its current status as one of the nation's most populous. As a chronicle of Florida brewing history *The Great Florida Craft Beer Guide* is impressively researched, enjoyable to read, and long overdue.

Cheers,
Joey Redner
Founder and CEO
Cigar City Brewing

Introduction

I was introduced to craft beer in 2004 at EPCOT's Food and Wine Festival. I still remember drinking Samuel Adams Cherry Wheat ale and the cherries giving me pause. I could not get over the taste. I then dabbled in craft beer with a few friends, but the epiphany came on November 15, 2008—a day in which three things happened that took me down the road to this book.

The first was that Stone Brewing Company of Escondido, California, launched its entrance into the Florida beer market with a great party at the Oldsmar Tap House in Oldsmar, Florida. While there were dozens of national craft breweries distributed in Florida already, Stone's beers, for me, had the flavor profiles I sought: immensely hoppy and very strong.

The second game-changer was a chance meeting and conversation with Joey Redner. The third was the realization that in founding Cigar City Brewing, Joey was doing something that had not been done in Tampa for about four decades: he was making and bottling Tampa beer in Tampa.

Then I met Wayne Wambles, the mad scientist. Wayne seemed a relatively quiet guy at first, but after I witnessed his palate and his hands at work, there was no other way to say it, Tampa was very blessed to have Wayne's expertise pouring into the tanks and the city. Wayne is Cigar City's first head brewer and he has made amazing beers. Ask him about his new centrifuge for lagers. Joey and Wayne have always made beers that I love to share and that I use to introduce friends and relatives to craft beer. The passion for craft beer that began for me on a sunny day in October 2004 has been fueled by Wayne and Joey's beer. That flame has caught and spread and now Florida is on pace to exceed fifty craft breweries in 2010 (by the time the book finished, the number is closer to one hundred). Many of these fledgling craft breweries came about after the success of Cigar City.

I honestly don't know whether it is the dedication of the craft brewers or the allure of this unique job and industry that gets the folks of Florida craft beer to work daily. Frankly, I don't care as long as they continue to drive Florida down the path of flavorful, hand-crafted, and locally made ales and lagers in years to come. Beer is not only about flavor and craft, in Florida (and I hope everywhere) it is about community. From its inception, Florida beer has been a celebration of endurance—turning the beer swamp that was Florida into a home, making beers that require refrigeration and storage in an age before commercial refrigeration, and creating something better for the people of Florida.

As the old adage goes, "Nature makes wine, but brewers make beer."

ABOUT BREWING: BASICS FROM GRAIN TO GOLD

While the brewing process, in layman's terms, involves the conversion of starchy sugars in a cereal grain into alcohol and carbon dioxide, a brewer looks at science as art. As a chef approaches cuisine, so too does a brewer approach beer. Beer contains four critical ingredients—water, grain, hops, and yeast—but can grow so far beyond the simplicity of its roots. Additional ingredients can be added at points in the brewing process, but the four core ingredients combine to form what has come to be known by civilization as beer. Many areas of the country have made short work of brewing because of the advantages that nature has given, but Florida has the opposite. Where Milwaukee has caves and cold winters, Florida has beaches and humidity.

The brewer begins with a mass of cereal grain, usually barley or wheat, and then soaks the grain in warm water to coax out the fermentable sugars and begin the beer-making process with a substance called wort, the tea-like mixture of grainy water. The more starchy sugars the brewer can get out of the grain, the more food the yeast have to devour in fermentation.

Next the brewer takes the wort and boils it, adding hops to the mixture at various points in the boil to impart hop aroma and bitterness to the finished beer. After the brewer both boils and hops the beer, it is then brought into fermentation tanks where endless possibilities begin to become reality. Once yeast is pitched on a beer, the microbes begin to eat the sugars in the wort and convert them into alcohol and carbon dioxide. Additional hops can then be added in a process called dry-hopping where the hops will add to the aroma of a beer, and additional ingredients can be added as the beer rests in fermentation. For example, if a brewer wants to highlight a stout's chocolate malt character by adding cacao nibs, then this is the usual part of the process where the addition will occur.

As the yeast continues its work, the beer becomes increasingly carbonated and will form a head when poured or give the tell-tale hissing sound when a bottle is opened. Once the beer is carbonated, it is moved from a fermenting tank into a brite tank (like a staging area) so that the brewer can move it into one of three package options: can, bottle, or keg. From the point a beer leaves a brewery, that beer could be many things to many people—it can become a special celebration bottle, a beer poured to a first-time beer-drinker at a festival, or a package shipped to a grocery store to slake the thirst of the everyday drinker. Whether for football, beach, or fiesta, beer embodies the spirit of both brewer and consumer: artful from golden grain to frothy fulfillment.

OPENING A BREWERY

Like a good beer, a brewery also needs time to develop richness and complexity when fermenting from an idea into a reality. Each brewery undergoes these phases, and while this book has tried to give mention of each brewery in Florida, many are advancing through the phases with each passing day.

Phase 1: Dreaming: "Wouldn't it be great to own and work in a brewery?" Friends converse over beers, home brewers imagine a reality where their hobby could become their occupation. This seems to be the most difficult step to transition through.

Phase 2: Financing: "Who's going to invest in my brewery?" At this time investors are secured and the dream begins to take shape. 3 Daughters Brewery used local investors, Bold City Brewery was born from 401K money, J. Wakefield Brewery in Miami crowd-funded, and 7venth Sun started small and uses profits to expand its operation. Secure jobs are abandoned, and leaps of faith take running starts. A physical space is selected and estimates obtained for transformation.

Phase 3: Permitting: "How can I legally run my brewery?" Appropriate permits must be obtained, and the brewery's workings and finances begin to take shape. Oftentimes, this step and the next step occur simultaneously.

Phase 4: Building: "What's this brewery going to look like?" The physical space is transformed into a working brewery. Plumbing, construction, equipment selection, and recipe construction can happen at this step. The building is then decorated to reflect theme. Dunedin Brewery is decorated with beers the brewery has bottled and bands that have toured there. Swamphead Brewery is decorated with cypress to reflect its swamp theme. Cigar City was festooned with bottles that the owner and his friends drank over the years. In each case, physical space is altered to give the brewery's best face.

Phase 5: Opening: "Let's invite everyone over to share our beer." This is the grand opening and beyond: distributors are chosen, people are hired, and beginnings begin. In the late 1800s, Tampa Florida Brewery took out a front page ad and invited everyone within the distribution area of the newspaper. First beers are tapped, anniversaries planned, and adventures begun.

A TOAST

This book is written in celebration of Florida's brewing community from 1896 to the present day. I raise my glass to the men and women who invested, risked, and achieved their dreams, even if only for a little while; and to all of the bar owners, distributors, brewers, and those who believed in craft beer and Florida beer before it was cool, let alone profitable, and generously shared their time, stories, and expertise. Florida beer has come a long way, has had some great help, and right now is in excellent hands.

The Earliest Florida Brew

Brewing in Tampa

TAMPA'S BREWING PAST

While Tampa can boast the oldest brewery in Florida, the story of Tampa's beer does not start the same way as every other spot in Florida. Like so much else about Tampa, beer started with a convergence of factors: a perfect storm of place, idea, men in motion, and financiers. History begins with a trickle of water coming up from the ground, feeding a spring in a thirsty area. This spring would be called Government Spring because it would come to slake the thirst of Fort Brooke, the command post on Tampa Bay and the seed that would sprout the City of Tampa. Here is where the story of Tampa's rich brewing history begins, with the most crucial of beer ingredients: water.

Origins

The Seminole Indian Wars were the first occasions that brought eminent military men to the Tampa area. Commanders the likes of Winfield Scott and Zachary Taylor, among other generals known to history, met at the spring with their men to plan their strategy. Since the founding of Fort Brooke, the whole of the property belonged to the United States government. Ownership of the spring would remain in government hands until 1882 when President Chester A. Arthur deeded the land to one of Tampa's founding families.

In 1886, the first cigar manufacturers moved into the Tampa area. The spring would then become part of "Mr. Ybor's City," as it was called in those days. In 1896, the same men with the keen business sense to bring cigars and labor to Tampa from Key West and Havana forged a new business for that same labor force.

Beer Begins to Flow

In 1896, the articles of incorporation of The Ybor City Brewing Company were filed with Tampa City Hall. The visionary founder, a former bookkeeper at the V. M. Ybor Cigar Company, had worked his way up from the lower echelon of the cigar company through the trust and friendship of Mr. Ybor. This man, Eduardo Manrara, had helped Ybor move his factory and his workers from Cuba to Key West and then voiced admiration for the climate of Tampa, one factor in the placement of Ybor's factory in what would come to be called Ybor City. Manrara was fifty-four years old when he organized the Florida Brewing Company, having already lived in Florida for eleven years and taken over the V. M. Ybor Cigar Company due to Ybor's failing health.

During the time when the idea of the brewery was being passed around and permits were being obtained, there was one notable force in the city of Tampa that fought the brewery's construction. More than those who sought to ban alcohol, the big breweries—Pabst Brewing, Schlitz Brewing, and Anheuser Busch Breweries—watched the new brewery with great concern. In the 1880s, Tampa was a town coming into its own, and many enterprising individuals had sought to increase their wealth by opening a saloon, a place where men could go to enjoy a quenching beverage and an intoxicatingly good time. As competition grew and the number of saloons increased, so did the costs associated with running saloons, including state fees and licenses. Saloons fought desperately to retain customers and pay their bills, but as the bills went up and the customers seemed to go elsewhere, the saloon owners sought relief anywhere they could find it. Pabst Brewing, Schlitz Brewing, and Anheuser-Busch Brewing spent untold thousands of dollars marketing in Tampa, tapping their coffers and pouring money out to saloons in exchange for exclusivity (a practice that is currently illegal and still alleged). They would pay a saloon owner's mortgage payments and licensing fees, essentially owning the saloon, but leaving the owner's name on the sign as a mere formality. Representatives of the big breweries knew who ran Ybor City and where the loyalties of the beer-consuming public would go when a brewery associated with their employer opened. They also recognized the considerable capital that came with the Ybor name, so resistance ultimately amounted to little in a town that bore Ybor's name and company. The large breweries never forgot Tampa, however. Though the Tampa foothold gained by the Saint Louis Breweries was washed out with the advent of the Florida Brewing Company, the companies would return in the mid-twentieth century; the rivalry would renew itself then, and the outcome would change the course of history for both companies.

When opening the brewery, Manrara and his associates had four major advantages. First was the sense of noblesse oblige that Ybor had toward all of his workers from the beginning of his cigar factories. In Ybor factories and across the cigar industry, it was considered acceptable practice for cigar rollers to take home a certain amount of their finished product as gratuity. Ybor was known for his strong dislike of organized labor and preference for one-on-one dealings with all of his employees. Ybor would throw parties annually for his workers on his palatial estate in Tampa and regularly provided for his workers in other ways. Second was Ybor's ownership of virtually every office in town. When Ybor founded his namesake town, he created, owned, or ran not just the cigar houses but also most of the other companies associated with the town, from the land development company to the fire insurance company. Hundreds of Ybor employees were housed in small shacks during the pioneer days of Florida history and were fiercely loyal. These men were not going to travel long distances for a libation, so the brewery essentially had a captive audience for its product. Third, the brewery had a direct well to Government Spring, which could deliver up to three hundred gallons per minute of the highest quality water. The final leg up that the brewery had before it even began brewing was Ybor's ties to other states and Cuba. The brewery was beginning as Ybor was declining, and the enterprises that Manrara assumed would all benefit from the ties that Ybor had created during his lifetime. Having established offices in Key West, Cuba, New York, and Tampa, Ybor had built relationships that proved invaluable to the Florida Brewing Company, especially as the brewery shipped massive amounts of beer to Cuba (more than any other brewery in America by 1900). The brewery was not just built from bricks and stones but by people and relationships, and all those close ties made the brewery a great idea before it even began.

From its early days, the Florida Brewing Company was illustrative of the period from which it came and the resourcefulness of its owners. With his cofounders E. W. Codington, Hugo Schwaub, and A. C. Moore, Eduardo Manrara started Florida's first brewery with two hundred thousand dollars capital stock. The brewery building was to be a technological marvel for its era, one that would spare little expense in production and construction during its sixty-plus years in operation, including continuous operation during the era of Prohibition. The brewery had a capacity of 30,000 beer barrels, in an era when the nation's largest brewers were brewing up to 800,000 beer barrels in Milwaukee and colder states. Unlike national breweries, Manrara and his associates did this with a lager beer (a beer that requires cold temperatures to ferment) in the southernmost state of the Union without the aid of Mother Nature. Lagers had drawbacks: lagers take longer to ferment raw materials into drinkable beer (the term *lager* comes from the German word "to store"), and most inconvenient of all in Florida, especially in a Florida where electrical infrastructure was still being developed, lagers must ferment at constant cold temperatures. After all, the reason these men came to Tampa was for the heat and humidity's aid in handling tobacco, not the cold seasons for beer brewing. This brewery stood, determined to succeed, despite Florida's unfavorable brewing weather.

When it opened on February 15, 1897, the Florida Brewing Company threw a grand party, the likes of which the city had not seen. For this celebration the brewery placed an ad on the front page of the local paper inviting "White or black, rich or poor" to come by for a day of merriment that included food, music, and beer. The opening celebration saw a landmark crowd descend upon the brewery, or so the food consumption would indicate. At the end of the day, twenty carcasses of barbecued beef, several barrels of pickles, and an estimated four hundred barrels of lager were consumed. With the exception of one person—a cigar worker who was struck on the head with a heavy ceramic beer mug after mistakenly drinking an ice plant worker's beer and was killed in the scuffle—the opening festivities were enjoyed by all present.

To say that the brewery operated on a grand scale would be an understatement. In an appraisal of the holdings of the Ybor Company written when V. M. Ybor died, the brewery was said to be fireproof (an assessment that would prove false) as well as constructed based on the Castle Brewery of South Africa. On the adjoining two acres, the company ran a $25,000 bottling works and a twenty-four-ton per day ice plant. The brewery operated cutting-edge machinery and De La Verne refrigerating machines to keep the brewery's cellars at a constant thirty-two degrees. From the first breath it drew, the brewery could produce two hundred barrels of beer per day, which if run overtime, could be increased to three hundred barrels. The brewery lowered some of its delivery costs by building a spur of the railroad directly to the property, and Manrara is quoted as saying that once the brewery could sell twenty barrels per day (at least one-tenth of capacity when the building opened), that any other monies would be profit. The appraiser recognized the fact that Ybor was diversely invested in virtually every aspect of the town and stated that there was not enough money in all of Tampa to convert the Ybor holdings into cash. The assessor then went further to make the boldest statement in the appraisal:

> The consequence of [owning so much of the town] is, to make all of these investments however diverse in their character, intimately dependent upon the activity and success of the factory. . . . Should the factory cease operations, real estate in Ybor City would shrink wonderfully in value, how much is impossible to predict . . . of the local investments, not one, except possibly the brewery in some future time, but would be seriously crippled.

In other words, the Florida Brewing Company was the only business of Ybor's that was not dependent solely on the cigar industry for its success or failure.

The dizzying growth that the Florida Brewing Company experienced before the twentieth century began is a testament to the thirsty people of Tampa and the tenacity of the brewery's owners. Aside from a few fires from which the brewery quickly recovered, the early years of the Florida Brewing Company were marked by expansion. The company proved to be like a mythological hydra: whenever a structure or machine burned, the company would swiftly replace it with something larger and more efficient. New machines were added, new buildings built, and new distribution was opened to Florida Brewing's beers.

When the battleship *Maine* was sunk in 1898 and America decided to send troops to Cuba during the Spanish-American War, Tampa was the launching point. In the spring and summer of 1898, Tampa hosted 66,000 soldiers bound for the island, and in 1899 the brewery began sending its beer to a now free Cuba. According to brewing journals of the day, in 1899 the brewery's board installed tanks that quadrupled beer production; the brewery had taken less than two years to outgrow itself. Soon after Tampa's beer arrived in Cuba, it was the most popular American brand on the island, and except for beer sold locally in Tampa, virtually all of the bottled beer made by the Florida Brewing Company went to Cuba.

By the beginning of the twentieth century, the Florida Brewing Company was enjoying unparalleled success. As the city was getting its first street lights, gas mains, and paved sidewalks, the brewery increased production threefold between 1897 and 1900—from a maximum of 4,000 barrels in 1897 to a maximum of 12,000 barrels in 1898. No better illustration of the brewery's prosperity stands than its float in the Labor Day Parade of 1900. Shaped as a giant barrel and filled with beer, the float was manned by Jim Mooney, who disbursed beer to thirsty parade-goers along the route down Franklin Street. At the end of the parade, it seemed that only the four horses pulling the carriage had not enjoyed the beer, as over 100 barrels of beer were shared with Tampans that Labor Day.

The ties that the Florida Brewing Company forged were ones that lasted as long as the brewery did. One of the relationships that the brewery built was with an enterprising individual and his small café. Casimiro Hernandez Sr. immigrated from Cuba and found work under Constantino Balbontin and the Florida Brewing Company. Balbontin would usually count on established saloons to sell the brewery's beers to the local community. In 1905, however, the brewery acquired a small café, which Hernandez joined as a partner. The cafe would have been close in design to a modern brewery's tasting room, since it was not unusual for a pre-Prohibition saloon to carry taps leaning more toward one brewery. Far from the hard-drinking and rough-talking saloons depicted in Hollywood movies, this café and others like it functioned more like a men's club or lively public house, where men who had left their families in the old country could seek employment, socialize, and converse over the news. Casimiro was known as a wise and generous man, and business was good at his establishment, the Columbia Café, which has grown to take its own place in Tampa history.

The Dark Times: National Prohibition

Dating back to the 1880s, the struggle for both temperance and prohibition had met with vehement and often flagrant resistance in Tampa. One prominent Prohibitionist minister referred to Tampa as "the most damnable wide-open and rottenest town this side of hell." This conflict was due, in part, to the cultures that helped to build and define early Tampa and Ybor City. The Latin cultures of Ybor City would often clash with the Protestant Tampans who advocated temperance for the entire city and organized for their cause. In 1885, Florida legislators added the nineteenth amendment to the state constitution allowing for a local option allowing each county in Florida the choice to permit the sale of liquor. In a referendum held in 1887, Hillsborough County voted to remain "wet." This election began a decades-long struggle between the forces for and against the prohibition of alcohol.

The conflicts between so-called wet and dry forces would continue until January 17, 1920. On this dark day for brewers across the United States, the Volstead Act took effect and nationwide prohibition of alcoholic beverages over 0.5 percent alcohol became the law of the land. Local stories tell of a great party the night before to be greeted by the sobering reality the next morning that there was literally no booze left to be purchased legally.

Some of Tampa's law-abiding citizens took Prohibition to heart and suffered for thirteen long years. However, many Tampans viewed the legalities of Prohibition as an option to be discarded in the right circumstances, and as such, Tampa was regarded by enforcement officials as one of the wettest cities in the United States.

Many of the large breweries across the country had to implement measures to save money and minimize expenses during Prohibition. Nationally, breweries resorted to selling yeast, vinegar, near beer (beer with little or no alcohol), and soda. One brewer, Yuengling Brewery of Pottsville, Pennsylvania (and later Tampa) invested in a creamery on its property, which proved locally successful and continued to operate until the 1980s. Many local breweries were not able to make some of the financial changes required for survival and were swallowed whole by the boogeymen of Prohibition, but fortunately that was not the case for the Florida Brewing Company.

While no one thrived during the dry days, many had the buffets of the 1920s softened. The largest force softening Prohibition's impact was corrupt politicians. Tampa remained "wet" in dry days because the city's governors, and in many cases police officers, were being monetarily persuaded to look the other way. Another force was the culture in Ybor City and the nature of enforcement. Prohibition historian Frank Alduino and Tampa historian Tony Pizzo explain enforcing the Volstead Act in Ybor City:

> In order to have a chance for a conviction, agents needed to arrest a defendant in the act of selling illegal liquor. In Ybor City, this was nearly impossible . . . every street corner in the city's Latin quarter had posted sentries that waited for federal agents. If one was spotted, a warning quickly spread throughout the neighborhood cafes, restaurants, and speakeasies. Since liquor was generally served in a pitcher, any evidence was simply destroyed by pouring it down the drain. When Prohibition agents arrived . . . they usually found patrons drinking nothing but café con leche.

Local legend also posits that underground tunnels were built that led from the brewery to the area where local gangster Charlie Wall held his speakeasies. Wall would have had more of a need for liquor than beer, and the brewery could have produced both, having purchased distillation equipment in 1909. The brewery was not able to sell beer legally, but it was still generating enough revenue from the Ice Works and Bottling company, along with any illegal operations to place advertisements for "Florida Export Health Drink" (near beer) in the local press. In an era when other breweries, national breweries, even large national breweries that had enjoyed astronomical success before Prohibition, were forced to cut expenses to the proverbial bone and get creative in revenue generation, the Florida Brewing Company still had an advertising budget and money to spend on promotion.

Tampa's longest-running restaurant, the Columbia Restaurant, confirms many of the theories about Prohibition in Tampa. In the restaurant's history book, the current generation recounts stories of Prohibition: "The Columbia's bartenders were never without work, but demitasse cups replaced shot glasses. Management still bought liquor; it was just more expensive and from less scrupulous distributors." The citizens of Ybor City were accustomed to alcohol and were willing to pay to continue these cultural traditions. The Columbia Restaurant and the owning families were deeply enmeshed in politics and generally got a few days notice before any raids. The alcohol was simply packed up and sent to the supply warehouse, where it rested until the raid had passed. Then they picked up with business as usual.

Although raids were occurring throughout Tampa, the answer to the Florida brewery's lack of financial woes came in the wake of a federal raid in 1924. When federal agents arrived at the brewery, they seized 12,600 gallons of beer; even though the beer was only the strength of modern light beer, it still surpassed the legal limit of the time. After the raid, the operating president of the company, Salvador Ybor, and the brewery manager, George Willis, were taken into custody, fined one thousand dollars for illegal activity, and sentenced to six months in jail for violation of the Volstead Act and attempting to bribe a federal officer (although local history says that Ybor went to Cuba and did not spend any time in jail). As agents dug deeper, Willis admitted that the brewery was still making beer, and the brewery's operations were temporarily closed. A New Orleans appellate court, however, overturned the case. If the brewery was making that much beer, there was a definite market for it somewhere in the city. Willis swore that he never attempted to bribe an official, but rather, he was solicited for a bribe. Once that accusation came to light, officials were reticent to take on the brewery again, and the brewery was able to make, sell, and transport its beers with relative ease.

By the early 1930s, Floridians in general and Tampans specifically decided that Prohibition, the "Noble Experiment," was out past its bedtime. The movement to repeal Prohibition began swiftly in the state and spread like wildfire. While the nation saw the reintroduction of beer into the national landscape on April 7, 1933, Floridians had to wait another month due to procedural red tape. Finally, after a veritable eternity, on May 8, 1933, Governor Sholtz signed a bill reintroducing beer to Florida. Tampa, one of the wettest dry cities in the country, could officially imbibe again.

Many Competitors Arrive, One Competes

With the departure of Prohibition, the Florida Brewing Company reopened and rechristened itself as the Tampa Florida Brewery, Inc. The new operation produced the beers that were the most popular in its day. As was the case in every other beer market in the United States at the time, German lagers were still what the people wanted, so that is what the Tampa Florida Brewery gave them. German lagers tend to have a relatively low alcohol content, so after several beers (depending on a person's weight, food and water intake, and time taken to consume said beers), the drinker might possibly not feel the effects of the alcohol the beer contained. The first and best-selling brand was a lager called La Tropical; its motto was "Taste Tells." In the case of the Florida Brewing Company, after considerable initial investments, the growth and popularity of its beer generally, and La Tropical specifically, the brewery's growth was able to fuel the needs and expenses of making the beer.

Prohibition's exit brought many enterprising individuals to fill the city's beer vacuum. S. J. Miller and Fred D. Schleifer were two such men who moved swiftly upon the repeal of Prohibition to build DeSoto Brewing Company to compete with the already established Tampa Florida Brewery. The men received a full-page article in the Tampa Daily Times on Christmas Eve of 1934, and they took out a full-page advertisement in addition to the article. DeSoto boasted the use of "German processes" and "certified hops from Czechoslovakia and Belgium [sic] malt in the making of DeSoto beer." The men also claimed that analysis of their water awarded them the "highest possible rating." The article also showed photos of the inner workings of the brewery; pipes leading to tanks which led to pumps that led to gauges which led to more equipment. If anything

La Tropical poster. Courtesy of Michael Zane.

was to be gleaned from the article, it was certain that DeSoto had plans to become an adamant fixture in Florida beer-making.

DeSoto Brewing has since become the Roanoke Island of historical Florida breweries; much was made of its arrival and then the brewery went silently into the night, never to be heard from again. Since city directories (phone books) are put together about a year in advance, DeSoto Brewing was listed in the 1935 city phone directory with a rich entry detailing five staff members and their positions, but the 1936 edition has a listing for only the brewery's address, and by 1937, nothing. In total, the brewery was around for about eighteen months, long enough to bottle some of its lager, but very little of the brewery survives.

One other brewery, the Fette Brewing Company, filed papers to become licensed as a brewery, but the operation was scrubbed before it could take off.

On the heels of DeSoto's opening came the October 1934 opening of Southern Brewing Company at 700 East Zack Street in Tampa. Southern Brewing was headed by two men, John A. Furlong, president, and Richard G. Jones, vice president and general manager, as listed in the city directory of 1935 (which would have been written circa 1934). The brewing operation opened with grand ambitions in an old dry goods warehouse. The brewery began with a capacity of 150 barrels per brewing session, and if it brewed around the clock, then it could brew up to five times each day. Complementary to the large brewing system, the bottling works could package up to 3,600 pints per hour on the line. The brewery also contained a glass-lined tap room so that patrons could both see the brewer at work and taste some of the freshest beer in Tampa.

From the beginning, Southern Brewing offered its flagship beer, Silver Bar (also known as SB Beer), a light 3.2 percent beer—one that would have been legal according to the amendment to the Volstead Act in 1934. Eventually, the brewers also made Old Tampa (lighter beer), Wurzburger Type (dark), Silver Bar Ale, and SB Bock.

Silver Bar poster. Courtesy of Michael Zane.

True to German roots, any ad for SB Bock would contain the German symbol for bock beer, the goat. SB Bock would be one of the first beers in Tampa to have a set release date—Saint Patrick's Day of every year.

After a brief expansion in 1937, Southern Brewing's sales seemed to slump until they took advantage of a golden opportunity. In 1938, the brewery participated in the Showman's Variety Jubilee, a beauty pageant in Atlantic City, New Jersey. In order to promote tourism to Florida, the brewery decorated a car and made the journey northward, stopping in every major Florida city. Once in New Jersey, the brewery's manager and advertising manager set up shop in the Hotel Madison, where all of the press was gathered for briefings and hospitality. The brewery's float even won second prize in the pageant's parade. The float included a giant pelican that laid an egg, which was then handed to the mayor of Atlantic City. Inside the egg lay salutations from Florida's mayors and samples of SB Beer.

From the beginning, one of the distinguishing features of Southern Brewing was the marketing acumen of the corporate officers. While Florida Brewing Company would best Southern Brewing Company in longevity and production, Southern Brewing managed to make their product, Silver Bar Beer, ubiquitous. From Tampa Electric's trolley cars that transported shoppers around Tampa to billboards around town, Silver Bar Ale would place an ad anywhere one would fit. In fact, the brewery would employ well-known cartoonist Oral Cloakey to draw cartoon advertisements for SB; one of those cartoons was so similar to a different cartoon that, in 1959, Walt and Roy Disney sent the brewery a letter threatening a lawsuit. Beginning in 1939, the brewery would execute several blitzkriegs of advertising, landing the brewery's name or products on each of the area's sixty-six radio broadcasts. If the advertising time was short on the radio, then a civic leader would sometimes thank the brewery for its support. The brewery used advertising for everything from "thank you" messages to the public to announcing release dates for new and seasonal beers. The brewery also deployed the image of the SB Girls: a young white woman sipping on a Silver Bar beer for white taverns and a young black girl sipping on an SB for black areas in segregated Tampa. As beer historian Michael Zane puts it, "SB's profits did not recognize a color barrier." Like constructing a good brew, if there was an advertising need then Southern Brewing crafted an ad to fill it.

After brewmaster Walter Heuer died in 1941, chemist Gene Warnstedt took the reins and steered the brewery through its most successful years in business. Like all Florida breweries during the World War II era, SB's business continued to increase. From 1943 to 1947, for example, Southern Brewing sold in excess of 90,000

Silver Bar advertisement. Courtesy of Michael Zane.

barrels of beer; increasing sales more than 30 percent over their previous banner years.

Southern Brewing would continue to innovate and expand in the early 1950s, converting bottling equipment to the in-vogue cone-top cans (a hybrid can/bottle made of canning materials but capped off like a bottle) and rolling out a new Silver Bar Premium Lager Beer in 1952. The brewery then converted to can beer in rolled cans and produced an exclusive run of Silver Bar rolled cans in different colors to collect as a set. Like a prize steer, Southern Brewing seemed to keep finding fertile grazing land throughout Florida.

The Road to Empire: Anheuser Busch's Second Coming to Tampa

In the late 1950s the brewery business as a whole was beginning to see an upswing as the children of Prohibition began to pass out of the market, and a new generation of consumers took hold. If the 1940s and early 1950s were an era of prosperity for Florida's breweries, then the late 1950s and early 1960s were the equivalent of the bubonic plague. As profits increased, national breweries began to explore the country for areas to expand, and several looked to add Tampa to their portfolio. The first company in line to do so was the Schlitz Brewing Company in 1956, much to the chagrin of the well-established local breweries.

The same year that Schlitz bought an empty brewery in Kansas City, Missouri, they broke ground on a plant in Tampa. The Tampa plant would be equipped only for canning, which was now the major focus of beer packaging. Southern Brewing was the company that would first be struck by Schlitz's lightning. In 1959, International Breweries of Detroit bought Southern Brewing. For a short while, the brewery conducted business without evidence of this change. International Breweries actually brought down recipes for beers brewed in northern areas and began releasing them in Florida, hoping to compete. Brands like Kol, Frankenmuth, Phoenix, Orbit, Stolz, and Bavarian beers all added to Southern's production, and International Breweries hoped these beers would buy them a chance to remain a contender. As Schlitz began to choke International Breweries out of market share, International Breweries renovated the Southern Brewing facility one last time.

In 1959 Anheuser Busch was certainly not the new kid in town, having sent its beer to Tampa since before Prohibition, but this arrival was different. This time, Anheuser brought staying power—this arrival would prove to be like the Galactic Empire's coming to Alderaan, an ominous shadow on the Treasure City.

In 1959 Anheuser Busch opened a beer garden and bird show adjacent to the Anheuser Busch Brewery. The large birdhouse was free, as was the beer served in the hospitality house. The hospitality house also offered a tour of the adjacent brewery. People came from miles around to see the birds and drink the beer; so many, in fact, that there are pictures of a 1964 tram system the company built in order to shuttle people effectively. Anheuser Busch began to favor this model of hospitality house with the brewery behind it. This plant was to become synonymous with Tampa; the road on which the gardens were located was soon given the beer maker's name, and Busch Boulevard would remain a major Tampa thoroughfare even beyond the closing of the namesake brewery in 1995.

With two Goliaths parading into town, the area breweries, although well established, were not prepared for the kind of beer brawl that would ensue. Schlitz and Anheuser's reemergence in Tampa would prove to be the back-breaking straw. Four years after the demise of Southern Brewing Company, the Tampa Florida Brewery decided to sell to International Brewers and Bottlers Corporation. As a final gasp after Tampa Florida Brewery folded, International Breweries purchased the rights to La Tropical, Tampa Florida Brewery's stalwart brand and began producing it at the Southern Brewing warehouse. They had hopes that La Tropical would somehow help them compete again, but like struggling against quicksand, the situation looked bleak. Southern Brewing finally gave up the frothy ghost in 1963, and International Breweries closed the plant on Zack Street.

The man who purchased both Southern Brewing and Florida Brewing Company for International Brewers and Bottlers, Samuel Greenberg, was interviewed in 1983 by a University of South Florida undergraduate student. Greenberg discussed the acquisition of Florida Brewing Company:

> There were still 100,000 barrels of beer in the brewery's storage tanks, [the company] kept some of the brewery's crew and began bottling the beer . . . the production of Florida Brewing Company with three men was 250 cans a minute. The current production of the Busch Brewery in 1961 was a smashing 1,000 cans per minute with one man running the machinery.

In the same interview, Greenberg also revealed the fate of the brewery's equipment. Tropicana of Cocoa Beach bought the brewery's pasteurizer, several South American breweries purchased tanks and equipment, and in a cruel twist of fate, the remainder of the storage tanks of the Tampa Florida Brewery were reconditioned and used to panel the VIP Room at the Anheuser facility in Tampa. When the same student interviewed Ted Schoenlein, the final brewmaster of the Florida Brewing Company, Schoenlein confirmed that Anheuser's competition was ultimately what closed the doors of the Florida Brewing Company from 1961 until 1999 renovations began.

Major Brewers and the Unlucky Building

While Anheuser-Busch was automating its production, the other major brewery in Tampa was also experiencing prosperity with local competition gone, but like a quiet night on the RMS *Titanic*, Schlitz's prosperity would not last. Schlitz's enduring contribution to Tampa would be a building that would adopt three more owners, for a total of four owners in forty years. Like Schlitz, two of the three owners would see their companies purchased or folded, and a millennium would turn before prosperity returned to this Tampa landmark.

In 1967, Meister Brau of Chicago introduced the concept of "lite" beer to consumers, and consumers embraced it with a full-body hug. In 1972, Miller Brewing Company purchased the "Lite" brand from Meister Brau and was poised to join the top three brewers in the country. Schlitz beers were already losing market share, and in 1973 the company turned to less expensive ingredients like hop extracts and corn syrup in hopes of saving their tumbling brands. As a cost-saving measure, Schlitz sold its Tampa plant to Pabst Brewing of Milwaukee in October of 1983. Pabst spent $8.5 million to acquire the building in the midst of its own economic woes.

In early 1986, facing plummeting sales nationwide and company-wide budget slashing from a new owner, Pabst Brewing ceased all operations at the 30th Street Tampa Plant. The plant employed 250 workers at that time, and all of them were put on a furlough until the company could regroup. Eventually, a small cadre of employees were called back to work in early April 1986. Pabst was hoping that new brands and strategic plant closures throughout the company would take the business off life support and into competition. Reality moved in an opposite direction, however, as the new owner died in 1987, and Pabst faced political problems from within, so the building was sold to Stroh Brewing for a $2.1 million loss. Stroh Brewing, based out of Detroit, Michigan, was enduring financial difficulties of its own. After it laid off all staff and sold the company, the brewery building on 30th Street passed into the hands of the Yuengling Brewing Company in early 1999.

The Home Brewing Revolution and a New Hope

With the advent of mass-produced light lagers and the admission that major breweries were using ingredients considered brewing adjuncts in their most popular beers, there began a strange sort of revolution in the early 1970s. At the same time that major brewers were focusing on making beers lighter, hobbyists from a plethora of backgrounds took to their basements and cellars, their garages and kitchens, and began attempting to create their own beers. They tweaked, they poured, they developed, and finally they began to sell their liquid wares to the public. Many of these men would become self-educated brewers, and many would meet entrepreneurs and change the course of beer in the twentieth century.

In 1967, entrepreneur and heir to the appliance fortune Fritz Maytag purchased the floundering Anchor Brewing Company of San Francisco, California—a move that would have lasting consequences for beer everywhere, including Tampa Bay. At a time when 124 brewing companies nationwide were operating 153 breweries, and the top four breweries owned one-third of the market, Anchor Brewing began producing and distributing beers like their Anchor Steam traditional beer.

This fire, begun in California, took time but ultimately began to spread. After the Tampa Florida Brewery and Southern Brewing lit a torch and suddenly perished, a local beer drought came about. Even though Budweiser, Pabst, Schlitz, and Stroh all took their turns producing beer in Tampa, these beers prided themselves on tasting the same all over the country, regardless of where they were brewed. The beers were uniform, and there were no beers unique to Tampa, merely other beers made in the area. Without local flavor and color the light of local beer shriveled into embers.

For Tampa, unique beers would come first at the hands of the Ybor City Brewing Company in 1994. More than thirty years after the closing of the Florida Brewing Company, Humberto Perez, a Venezuelan businessman from a brewing background, decided to invest $2.6 million in the renovation of the 36,000-square-foot Seidenberg and Company cigar factory in Ybor City. In the large three-story brick building, Perez installed equipment for making up to 60,000 barrels of beer annually. Ybor City Brewing Company began its 1994 brewing profile by introducing its core beer, Ybor Gold Lager, into Tampa. The launch came at a time when the Anheuser plant in Tampa was making 6 million barrels of beer annually, and small brewers like Ybor City Brewing comprised only 0.03 percent of the beer market in the United States. The rest belonged to monoliths like Anheuser-Busch, Miller, and Coors (the last two would merge in 2007), whose history and profitability made brewery startup a herculean task.

Ybor City Brewing Company would enjoy a brief success in the Tampa and Florida markets. The company expanded its beer profile by adding a wheat beer, dubbed Calusa Wheat, in June of 1995, and an English-style brown ale, dubbed Ybor Brown, also in 1995. An article in the local paper and fanfare greeted each beer. Perez encountered issues with his distributor at the time, and according to an article in a local business paper, the local Budweiser distributor was incentivized by Budweiser corporate office not to sell Ybor City Brewing Company's beer. It took time to get the brewery's beer to a different distributor, and by that time the brewery had lost a large number of sales. Despite success for a microbrewery at the time, Perez saw his brewery's stars become crossed after the distributor troubles. Perez decided to close the brewery yet continue to brew Ybor City's beers—since he was also president of the Melbourne-based Florida Beer Company, Perez sold Ybor City Brewing's recipes to Florida Beer Company, which still brews them today, in a limited capacity, at its state-of-the-art Port Canaveral Brewery.

Lasting Legacy of Ybor City Brewing

If the large breweries had put up a wall against competition, then Ybor City Brewing Company's lasting legacy was to crack that wall. Not so deep as a well, nor so wide as a church door, but just enough. Ybor City Brewing Company filled the void of local beer that passed with Tampa Florida Brewery and Southern Brewing of old Tampa, and it took up the banner of making flavorful, locally inspired beers. The Ybor City Brewery brewed a beer for Tampa's annual Gasparilla Festival, a Tampa tradition for decades, which commemorates Jose Gaspar and his band of pirates "invading" Tampa. The company brewed a beer commemorating the Calusa peoples—native peoples who lived in the Tampa Bay area for centuries, long before European settlers. It brought people out of their homes and gave them a story to tell with its beer. It tied the beer to local culture and traditions in a way that seemed to pass out of memory, and grew clear roots in Tampa.

Around the same time Ybor City Brewing Company was working to establish itself, right down the street from the brewery was a nascent home brew shop run by the Doble family. The family conferred and dreamed of a place where great food and great beer could mix together. The pub would later be called Tampa Bay Brewing Company, and in the twenty-first century would move locations across Ybor City to become a fixture in Centro Ybor.

Across Tampa Bay in Dunedin, home brewers were working out recipes to bring forth the same kind of brewery and pub in the small artsy community of Dunedin. There home brewer Michael Bryant would look for a place where other home brewers could work with professional brewers and develop great beer recipes. A small facility was purchased and core beers were established. The pub would later be called the Dunedin Brewery and near the turn of the century would move to its current location on Douglas Avenue adjacent to the bay breeze.

In Clearwater, the early 1990s saw the advent of a pub called Hops that would serve American fare with the addition of house-brewed beers. While that concept is not a new one, for the time, it was well received. Hops grew from one restaurant to thirteen in the span of five years, and served as another step that helped beer and brewers in Tampa ferment into their current state. After the trail was blazed, other breweries came in and helped to lay down stones. New World Brewery in Ybor City opened, Hoppers brewpub opened in Palm Harbor, and after 2000, Saint Sebastien Brewery of Belgium decided to open a satellite pub in Spring Hill in Hernando County. While not all of these breweries would succeed, all of these forebears helped lay asphalt on the path Tampa's next generation of breweries would walk on. From Bob Sylvester's opening Saint Somewhere Brewing in Tarpon Springs to make Belgian-style farmhouse ales to Joey Redner's opening Cigar City Brewing to help bottle Tampa's history in the form of malt beverages, all of them are standing on the shoulders of Tampa's first brewers, going back to 1896.

What these pubs brought were also intangibles, like opportunities for people interested in beer to learn from people established in making beer. During this time a mindset and ethic evolved that still exists in the Tampa Bay beer market: the mindset that brewers and breweries are in the market together, not as competition against each other but as a family that helps each other, and when one brewery has a success, everyone is better for it.

Dunedin Brewery

Brewery/Brewpub
937 Douglas Avenue, Dunedin 34698
(727) 736-0606
http://dunedinbrewery.com
Open 7 days a week

A mainstay of the Tampa Bay beer scene, Dunedin Brewery is a cozy pub that looks like it should have been a small firehouse. In here, only the bar divides patrons and the brewing tanks and the pub resonates with the smell of malted barley and freshly poured beers. On any given evening, the brewery will have a band playing, a guitarist singing, or a drum circle drumming. In the past few years, the brewery expanded its facility to add the Nook Bar around the corner

(under the same roof) from the existing bar, in order to expand tap selection and offer more seating. With the additional space and the brewery's increasingly experimental and more hop-forward beers, Dunedin Brewery is a great stop during a day in the Dunedin area.

The story of the Dunedin Brewery is the story of the Bryant family. Owner Michael Bryant began home brewing in the 1980s and '90s and perfected his recipes until he was on the cusp of becoming a professional brewer. He opened Dunedin Brewery in 1996 as a place to build community through beer. The brewery opened with a small seven-barrel brewing system, and since moving to the new brewery in 2001, it currently has a capacity of 3,000 barrels. It is currently brewing at about 30 percent of capacity and working hard to keep up with demand for their beers. The brewery packages most of its beer in kegs with a portion of selected beers going into swing-top bottles for sale only at the brewery.

The Dunedin Brewery features seven year-round beers: Celtic Gold, Apricot Peach Wheat, Wheat Ale, Redhead Red, Piper's Pale Ale, Beach Tale Brown Ale, and Nitro Stout. In addition to its core lineup, the brewery also pours seasonal beers that change on a monthly basis and run the gamut of beer styles. February sees the premiere of Leonard Croon's Old Mean Stout, April offers a beer made specifically for the highland games, usually a scotch ale, and May welcomes the sweet and strong Local Honey Ale. June begins lager season with a maibock and blond pilsner while July brings in the Anniversary Bohemian Pilsner and September greets the Oktoberfest. October opens with a pumpkin beer, and November and December ring in Blitzen's Cinnamon, Honey, and Orange Ale for Christmas time.

Insider Tip: Dunedin Brewery throws several beer-style focused events each year. Look for Stogies and Stouts, Summer IPA Festival, Spring Jam, and Oktobeerfest to showcase seasonal and noteworthy beers.

Tampa Bay Brewing Company

Brewpub
1600 East 8th Avenue, Tampa 33605
(813) 247-1422
http://tampabaybrewingcompany.com
Open 7 days a week

Historic Centro Ybor, the central building in Ybor City, has in its heart Tampa Bay Brewing Company. The brewery occupies one corner of the restaurant, including the canning line used to can Old Elephant Foot, the brewery's flagship IPA. Patrons can watch the brewery in motion at lunchtime, and enjoy a beer brewed not thirty feet from where they sit.

The brewing company began as a supply store for local home brewers in 1994, and the Doble family decided to expand operations into a brewpub in 1996. The brewery has grown with the community and after the brewpub grew too big for its home on 15th Street, the larger pub was built in Centro Ybor in 2006. (The previous site is now home to Cigar City Cider and Mead.) The beer has been flowing in Ybor City ever since, and the brewery cannot seem to brew enough IPA for its thirsty patrons.

Head brewer Dave Doble says that Tampa Bay Brewing Company's beers are classic yet assertive representatives of their style. The pub will have the eight core beers on at all times: True Blonde Ale, One Night Stand Pale Ale; Wild Warthog Weizen; roasty and coffee-minded Jack the Quaffer Porter; the chocolate and cocoa tasting Iron Rat Imperial Stout; a hoppy red, Red Eye Red Ale; assertively hoppy Old Elephant Foot IPA; and the sweet Moose Killer Barleywine. Along with the core beers, there are at least two taps and a cask for the brewery to put into play at any given time. There could be anything from an imperial pilsner to a smoked scotch ale

rotating through the seasonal taps. The brewery also sells cans to go and is distributed throughout Pinellas and Hillsborough Counties, in addition to a small portion in Pasco and Sarasota Counties. The brewery is working hard to meet demand for its beers, and was recently featured on Food Network's *Diners, Drive-ins, and Dives* to showcase the pub's food.

The Tampa Bay Brewing Company is always worth a stop for a bite and a beer. Much of their food is prepared with beer and they strive to incorporate their beer into all aspects of the pub. Everyone who works there undergoes a training to be able to talk their way through the beer, and the longer someone has worked there, the more experience they have with the beer. Like all good craft breweries, they rotate their tap list so something new and exciting is always on draft and like a minuteman, their cans are ready to go home with anyone on a moment's notice.

Insider Tip: Tampa Bay Brewing Company works to tap a new cask beer every Thursday. These can be either casks of existing beers, dry-hopped beers, or treatments of existing TBBC beers.

Tampa Bay Brewing Company's recent expansion includes a $5 million dollar production brewery and restaurant in the Westchase area.

Yuengling Brewery

Brewery
11111 North 30th Street, Tampa 33612
(813) 972-8500
http://yuengling.com
Tours offered at various times. Gift shop is open Monday through
 Saturday.

The Yuengling Brewery near USF is the largest producer of craft beer in Florida. This bustling monolith is part of Yuengling, the oldest brewery in the United States, dating back to 1829, almost as old as Fort Brooke, the military outpost that would become Tampa. The plant itself is several stories tall and has a leg of the railroad connected to it for supply delivery. The brewery hosts the adjacent hospitality house where patrons can sample several of Yuengling's beers after a tour and hear the history of both the company and the brewery's building.

The Yuengling brand originates in Pottsdam, Pennsylvania, but in 1999, as part of an expansion project, company owner Dick Yuengling bought the then-abandoned Stroh's brewery on North 30th Street in Tampa. Because brewing beer is such a specialized art, and there were hundreds of employees who had been recently laid off by Stroh's, Yuengling called up and attempted to rehire the employees who had lost their jobs. Yuengling was able to rehire

much of the former Stroh plant and put hundreds of people back to work. He also did not have the added disadvantage of dealing with the competition of a Budweiser Brewery right down the street, as the Budweiser plant closed down four years before Yuengling moved in.

Almost the entire Yuengling beer line is available to taste after the Yuengling brewery tour, which is free to the public. Yuengling's core brands, its lager, premium, porter, black and tan, light lager, ale, and light ale are almost always available for tasting, and seasonals like bock and Oktoberfest are available when they're in season.

The Yuengling tour takes about an hour and fifteen minutes and goes over the brewing process from start to finish, the ingredients used, and the people involved. The tap room and gift shop are nice areas to compare notes about Yuengling's line of lagers and ales and meet people from all walks of life. Touring Yuengling is different than touring almost any other facility in Florida—it is Florida's largest beer-maker and its volume and automation while still attending to the flavor and quality of the beer make this facility worth a stop.

Cigar City Brewing

Brewery
3924 West Spruce Street, Tampa 33607
(813) 348-6363
http://cigarcitybrewing.com
Tasting room open 7 days a week
Tours offered on various days at various times; $5 per person
(includes a beer); reservations online

Cigar City is one of the breweries that put Tampa and Florida on the beer map. Cigar City was Tampa's first production-minded craft brewery, the first to start from the ground floor and focus on bottling and distribution outside its facility. This massive and ever-growing facility is located just south of the stadium where the Buccaneers play and behind a plaza with Whole Foods and Home Depot. The brewery's tasting room pours most of its liquid wares and offers bottles and growlers to go.

Cigar City's founder and owner, Joey Redner, initially did not plan on opening a craft brewery. He planned to wait until someone else opened one then he planned to work for the other guy. He began by working for the Dunedin Brewery, operating a pub, and working other jobs before securing the current facility on Spruce Street. Once the brewery was underway and head brewer Wayne Wambles was brought on board, the brewery's offerings began to expand greatly, including a thick and viscous imperial stout that is only offered for sale at the brewery one day each year.

Cigar City makes its core beers year round, including Jai Alai IPA, Maduro Brown Ale, and Tocobaga Red Ale. Cycling seasonals also appear from time to time, like White Oak–aged Jai Alai IPA, Cubano-style Espresso Brown Ale, Jose Marti American Porter, Bolita Double Nut Brown Ale, Guava Grove Farmhouse Ale, Improv Oatmeal Rye India-style Brown Ale, Big Sound Scotch Ale, Sugar Plum

Brown Ale, Marshal Zhukov's Imperial Stout, and Good Gourd Imperial Pumpkin Ale. In addition to the monumental lineup are the 110K+OT Series (bold, brash, and braggadocious beers), Capricho Oscuro Series (blending barrel-aged beers), Humidor Series (beers aged on cedar), and Criterium Series (beers brewed for the annual Tampa Criterium race), which have similar ideas behind them, but each incarnation differs from the last. If all that was not enough, the brewers also create pilot system beers and test batch beers that appear on draft at various times throughout the month.

Cigar City is unique to Tampa and has come a long way since opening its doors in 2009. The brewery began at one end of an industrial plaza and has moved to take over the entire plaza. The operation started with two people and is now approaching fifty employees. No matter how much the brewery grows, it tries hard to remain true to its roots and not only make great beer but also incorporate Tampa's history into the story of the beer.

Insider tip: Cigar City Brewing does not always post all bottles for sale in the tasting room on social media. In fact, they like to surprise locals by placing rare and barrel-aged beers for sale randomly. Always look thoroughly at the bottle cooler.

Cigar City Brewpub

Brewpub
15491 North Dale Mabry Highway, Tampa 33618
(813) 962-1274
http://www.cigarcitybrewpub.com/
Open 7 days a week

The Cigar City Brewpub is housed in a restaurant that used to be a T.G.I. Friday's in the Northdale area of Tampa. The brewpub is an outgrowth of the brewery and has the same attention to detail in the restaurant that the brewery puts into its beers. From chandeliers molded with beer bottles and cans to can tops lining the bar, from areas paneled with barrel wood to pictures of Cigar City employees throughout the dining area, this brewpub took Cigar City's history and philosophy and paired it with great food to produce an exceptional experience.

The Cigar City Brewpub is located immediately off Dale Mabry Highway in the Northdale section of Carrollwood. The brewpub pairs a world-class chef and a world-class brewer and takes patrons along for the ride. While the restaurant is owned by the brewery and some of the taps are supplemented by beers from the mother brewery on Spruce Street, the beer brewed at the brewpub differs from Cigar City's offerings. The brewpub's brewer is Tim Ogden, the veteran brewer who brought the world Cigar City's Tocobaga Red Ale. The brewpub gives Tim time and space to turn out beers to his taste with the panache of Cigar City.

While the Cigar City Brewpub's small brewing system will allow for small batch ales in limited runs, the brewpub core offerings are

the floral La Rubia Golden Ale, the earthy and molasses-forward Paulina Pedrosa Brown Ale, and the fruity, yet bitter Northdale Pale Ale. The brewpub's brewing system is also fuel for the Floridian collaborative spirit. Other Florida breweries like Funky Buddha, Saint Somewhere, Gravity Brewlab, and Angry Chair Brewing have all come in and brewed with Ogden. Also look for cask beers and limited run beers available only at the pub.

The concept of the Cigar City Brewpub is simple: take food from the local market and support neighboring businesses and farms while brewing beer feet away from the tables where it will be enjoyed. While visiting the pub, don't miss the plantain tater tots or the house special Hunahpu dessert. On a good night, there exists a culinary unicorn of a meal: the freshest beer and the freshest food creating a perfect storm of localvore dinner.

Insider Tip: Tim Ogden's Brewer's Brunch Stout and Gourds of Thunder are two seasonal beers not to be missed. Brewer's Brunch makes fleeting appearances, but Gourds of Thunder is the brewpub's Thanksgiving/Halloween beer. Both beers stand apart from others of their kind.

Peg's Cantina

Brewpub
3038 Beach Boulevard, Gulfport 33707
(727) 328-2720
http://pegscantina.com
Hours are seasonal; closed Monday and Tuesday

Peg's Cantina is a laid-back little eatery on the main strip of Gulfport in southern Pinellas County. Peg's serves pizza and Mexican food next to its house-made beers. The tiny environs inside Peg's provide a haven from the weather and the large front patio allows patrons to relax and watch everyone else bustle by. Peg's focuses on local and organic foods as much as possible and insists on being "a public space that [brings] folks together to share food, drink, and fun."

Peg's Cantina is family owned by Peg and Tony Dozark, who were both academics in their past lives. They were lured away from academic lives in New York by the Florida sunrise and decided to open a little place in their hometown of Gulfport. Their son, Doug, began brewing, and they got licensed to serve his beer. Doug then continued to hone his talents as a brewer at Cigar City by day and Peg's by night, so as Doug's reputation grew, Peg's expanded its brewing operations.

As Peg's head brewer, Doug Dozark has a true rotating tap list as there is no telling what will be on draft at any given time. Doug almost always has something light, like his 99 percent lager, something hoppy, like his Dancing Cody IPA, and something dark, like

his El Dude Porter or Bottom of the Ninth Brown Ale. Doug also has a passion for light and refreshing beers and in 2012 began hosting the Berliner Bash on the Bay, an event where brewers from around the state can showcase their renditions of a tart wheat beer called a Berliner weisse. Periodically Doug will mix up his tap selection with his Bloody Berliner (a beer that crosses a Bloody Mary and a tart wheat beer) or Rainbow Jelly Donut Berliner (a beer that crosses a raspberry donut with a tart wheat beer). In Peg's Cantina or Gulfport itself, there's no telling what may turn up on the draft list.

As Doug's talent and penchant for making great beers continues to grow, so too does Peg's reputation. The cantina has been recognized nationally by several newspapers and websites as a unique place to visit, eat, and drink. As the beer scene grows in Tampa and Florida, it is hoped more places will follow Peg's model and maintain an easy-going place to sit, eat, and have a beer, but until that point, there is no place like the original.

Insider Tip: Look for Peg's to get a few kegs when Cycle Brewing hosts special events like Barrel-aged Day or Share the Barrels.

Cycle Brewing Company

Brewery
534 Central Avenue, Saint Petersburg 33701
(727) 320-7954
Open 7 days a week

Cycle Brewing is the natural outgrowth of Doug Dozark's brewing career, which began at both Peg's Cantina and Cigar City Brewing. After an internship at Cigar City, Doug was one of the first hires beyond owner Joey Redner and brewer Wayne Wambles. Doug has grown and progressed to brewing solely at Peg's, but a capacity ceiling at Peg's combined with a desire to blaze his own trail led Doug to begin a brewing endeavor all his own: Cycle Brewing.

Many of Doug's ideas that began at Peg's Cantina continue to blossom at Cycle Brewing; in fact, when Doug announced the surprise opening on Facebook in August of 2013, he was technically the head brewer at two locations, a tradition that he continues. At Cycle, Doug is able to craft his beers on a seven-barrel brewing system with seven-barrel fermenters, supplying his taps and a few select accounts with Cycle beer.

Low-alcohol, hop-intense IPAs, like his Fixie American Session Ale and Freewheel Pale Ale will take up residence on Cycle's draft board alongside intensely coffee-forward Cream and Sugar Please. Occasional tap visitors include Bottom of the Ninth Brown Ale, a malty brown ale, The Dude Porter, a chocolate and coffee-forward porter, and Ryerish Red, an Irish Red Ale with the malt character of a red ale and hints of spicy rye to complement. When Tampa Bay Ray Evan Longoria invested in a lounge called Ducky's, Cycle was sought out to brew the namesake pilsner for its taps. Cycle also devotes space to the occasional visitors to the tap list: Doug's barrel-aged and sour offerings. In fact, for several weeks after opening Cycle rotated through Rare D.O.S. (bourbon barrel–aged Doug's Original Stout), RareR D.O.S. (rum barrel–aged Doug's Original Stout), Hazelnut Rare D.O.S., and other elusive liquid treats. The lines in the new tasting room shouldn't get too long—seating flows outside on Florida days, and inside is approved for a maximum of only forty-nine people.

Doug's success at Peg's Cantina has allowed him the creative license and following to open Cycle Brewing, and Doug is intent on making Cycle a success, too, and to keep both his tap room and his parents' restaurant full of beer. Look to Cycle for consistent surprises—Cycle's opening was announced on Facebook after several days of construction updates and came as a surprise to the local community.

Insider Tip: Cycle Brewing is cash only. Bring your own, or there are several ATMs within walking distance.

Green Bench Brewing Company

Brewery
1133 Baum Avenue North, Saint Petersburg 33705
(727) 800-9836
http://www.greenbenchbrewing.com
Closed Monday

Another craft brewery blazing its way to the forefront of Saint Petersburg's craft beer revolution is Green Bench Brewing Company. Green Bench is the brainchild of owners Steven Duffy and Nathan Stonecipher with Khris Johnson, a home brewer turned professional after stints at Cigar City Brewing and Southern Brewing and Winemaking. Khris has been keeping busy since Green Bench began construction in March of 2013. In addition to brewing, Khris works on Green Bench's social media presence and fields many questions about Green Bench and the beers coming forth. The brewery's production facility and tasting room boast several Saint Petersburg firsts and one of the greenest lawns in the downtown area.

Green Bench Brewing is named after the iconic green benches that used to line the streets of Saint Petersburg around the turn

of the twentieth century. The benches became associated with the Saint Petersburg of yesteryear, and as the brewery puts it, "invit[ed] passers-by to slow their pace and make friends of strangers. In the same way Green Bench beer will serve as a catalyst for community and cheer." How dedicated is this brewery to making local beer in the city of Al Capone and Jack Kerouac? So dedicated that brewery personnel worked with the folks at the City of Saint Petersburg Zoning Commission and they rewrote some of the local code in order that a brewery could take up residence and do business. Before Green Bench Brewing came along, Saint Petersburg was unequipped to handle all of the breweries eyeing the city's untapped market. Now, thanks to Green Bench, the taps can flow from breweries and tasting rooms alike all over the county.

Green Bench Brewing Company plans to perfect its lineup of core beers and seasonal/rotational offerings as the owners get to know their market. On the first day of business, September 25, 2013, they begin with five beers: Green Bench IPA, Maximo Milk

Stout, Temple Mound Brown Ale, Skyway Wheat, and Saison de Banc Vert. Khris has plans for twelve to fifteen different brews produced in Green Bench's first year of operation. Johnson also began working with 100 percent oak fermentation and a unique line of Belgian beers, different than anyone has experienced thanks to their foeders. Johnson adds that his Belgians will have an "added complexity." At the end of the day, Johnson says that he wants to focus on drinkability and balance but tread the line of extreme flavors. He wants beer to be an experience from start to finish.

Insider Tip: Green Bench is addressed on Baum Ave. The GPS may send you by way of First Avenue North, but tasting room access is much better on Baum Avenue. Look for the lawn.

Rapp Brewing Company

Brewery
10930 Endeavour Way, Suite C, Seminole 33777
(727) 692-7912
http://rappbrewing.com
Open 7 days a week

Rapp Brewing is owned by award-winning home brewer and founder of Pinellas Urban Brewers' Guild, Greg Rapp. Operating out of a warehouse space off the main vein in Seminole, near Largo, Rapp Brewing is hard at work making central Pinellas County a beer destination for all of Florida.

Brewery owner Greg Rapp and his wife began this project in 2012 and have been pouring at beer festivals throughout the Tampa area in order to drum up support for the brewery and beers they produce. Greg has brewed virtually every style of beer as a home brewer and has transitioned to commercial brewing on a small 1.5-barrel brewhouse. Greg is focusing on every detail of his beer, and to that end he installed a 200-gallon per day reverse osmosis water filtration system so that he can simulate the water profile of

almost any brewing city in the world. The water filtration allows him to use Pinellas County's water to create beers similar to other global cities (like Pilsen for pilsners) and make geographically different beers without leaving Florida.

Rapp Brewing Company is excited about producing lagers and ales, traditional ales, and beers for people who are not as experienced in the realm of craft beer. Rapp's core beers are a Leipzinger Gose, a Berliner weisse, and constantly rotating taps. Rapp brews any number of beers, from a peanut butter stout to an imperial IPA to a scotch ale. The brewery may be small, but Rapp's resume and recipe book are certainly not. In fact, Rapp has been keeping a log—he has brewed and served fifty-nine different beer styles in sixteen months.

Greg envisions making the brewery as big as the community will help it become. With every bottle release and every new beer, the small brewery gains popularity and notoriety and Rapp never travels lightly. After all, to every festival that Rapp Brewing Company has attended, he has brought at least eight beers, with very few repeats.

One thing is for certain: with a small brewhouse and quick turnaround, the constant at Rapp is a plethora of different beers, including Rapp's signature strong ale, OMG, which was Rapp's first bottle release. Rapp is still a destination brewery, but distributes in a limited fashion around the Tampa Bay Area.

Insider Tip: Rapp releases his OMG beer in batches sporadically. Keep an eye on social media for the next release.

Pair O Dice Brewing Company

Brewery
4400 118th Avenue North, Suite 208, Clearwater 33762
(727) 755-3423
http://pairodicebrewing.com
Closed Monday through Wednesday

One of Pinellas County's newest breweries on the outskirts of Saint Petersburg, which can claim the title of Clearwater's first craft brewery despite barely residing in that city, is Pair O Dice Brewing. Pair O Dice is run by husband and wife Ken and Julia Rosenthal. They see Florida as paradise, themselves as a pair, the dice as taking a chance, and the beer as what joins all of the above together in their 8,700-square-foot brewery.

Ken and Julia began their experience in the beer community in an unlikely place: both used to work for Anheuser-Busch. Ken became a home brewer in 2004, and after six years, he turned professional. Ken insists that his tenure at Anheuser Busch combined with his taste for fresh and flavorful beers gave him the drive to produce quality and flavorful American beers with the consistency and attention to detail of a craft brewer. Ken and Julia's time together after Anheuser-Busch planted the seeds of becoming craft brewers when they saw the explosion of craft creativity in Austin, Texas. After exploring the Austin craft beer experience, Ken and Julia decided to roll the proverbial dice and open a brewery on the west coast of Florida.

Pair O Dice focuses on traditional, American craft ales and lagers. Ken enjoys beer more toward the dry side, but his brewing philosophy focuses on fresh, local, and balanced styles of beer. Pair O Dice's current beers include Parlay Pale Ale, Hop Bet Red Ale, and Little Joe Oatmeal Stout. The Clearwater brewery's tasting room pours from twenty taps and focuses on showcasing beers from kindred Florida brewers. From there, Pair O Dice Brewing has plans to produce beer enough to spread across Florida.

Sea Dog Brewing Company

Brewpub
26200 US Highway 19 North, Clearwater 33761
(727) 466-4916
http://www.seadogbrewing.com
Closed Monday and Tuesday

After several attempts at carving a foothold into Florida, Shipyard Brewing Company, under the cute and loveable guise of Sea Dog Brewing, staked their claim in Pinellas County. The Maine brewery was bound and determined to join Florida's "more than a snowbird" population and ended up doubling down and upping the stakes on their southernmost expedition.

The Sea Dog Brewing Company of Clearwater opened its doors in February of 2013 as a restaurant serving Shipyard's signature beers with ambitions of becoming a brewpub. The bright and airy pub got by for a while using Shipyard and Sea Dog beers, but the community was looking for more house beers—Florida beers made within Florida. Up to this point, the brewpub had been utilizing a smaller system to produce house beers and barrel-aged novelties for pub consumption. Head brewer Bobby Baker wasted no time producing unique beers the likes of which Clearwater had never seen: Raspberry Stout, Drunken Honey Sour, Sand Dollar IPA, and Reef Monster Blood Orange Wheat Ale.

Floridians, however, sounded a call for a larger brewing operation, and Sea Dog responded with vim and vigor. Maine declared that the brewpub would sacrifice some patio space in exchange for a twenty-barrel brewing system. At the same time, Pinellas County loosened restrictions on craft brewers, allowing businesses zoned as "light manufacturing" to sell alcohol. The brewpub immediately got to work converting patio space into the future of Sea Dog and Shipyard operations in Florida—space that would eventually house brewing vessels and a canning line. The coup de théâtre was the resurrection of the Shipyard brewing system, which had brought Shipyard's freshest beers to the Orlando International Airport, from its cargo-crate grave back into brewing service.

Construction was completed, and the new Sea Dog system was primed and ready with an opening date of April 10, 2014. On April 1, 2014, Baker got his hands on the system and took it for a spin. What had once begun as a noisy patio packed with the dissonance of Clearwater's busiest traffic suddenly became a libation oasis producing beers for Pinellas County and beyond. Florida in general and Pinellas specifically now had a place to enjoy Maine-inspired food and beer with a Florida twist: a salute to both snowbirds and year-long locals alike, much like Florida itself.

Brewery
1012 Broadway, Dunedin 34698
(727)733-3013
http://www.7venthsun.com
Closed Monday

7venth (Seventh) Sun Brewery opened its doors in January of 2012 and has been growing ever since. The brewery and tasting room is located in a small plaza adjacent to State Road 580 and Alternate 19 in Dunedin. The tiny brewery has a few seats inside, a few seats outside, and ten taps touting tantalizing brews. If ever there was a brewery that could warn people not to judge the beer by the size of

the tap room, 7venth Sun is the poster child. After an initial opening and subsequent growth, 7venth Sun moved into an additional unit to allow more seating while maintaining its cozy confines.

Brewer Justin Stange and Devon Kreps founded 7venth Sun Brewery. Justin is a brewing alumnus of Georgia's Sweetwater Brewery and Tampa's Cigar City Brewing. While he worked for other people, he was busy perfecting his own recipes and working to build a facility in a small space in the artsy community of Dunedin. The brewery's Facebook page features pictures of Justin and Devon doing much of the construction for 7venth Sun by themselves, including building the bar in front of the house's hand-blown glass taps. 7venth Sun releases bottles of its beer from time to time, but it is usually a small run and oftentimes the brewery has more people looking for bottles than they have bottles.

Justin tries to keep at least five house beers on tap at all times at 7venth Sun, and with an expansion nearly doubling capacity in January of 2013, he can almost keep up with demand. He brews the kinds of beers that he likes to drink, and he has eclectic tastes. 7venth Sun will always have something hoppy, something easy-drinking, and something Belgian on tap, if he can keep up with the beer-drinking populace. Justin rotates his IPA recipe seasonally, so each IPA recipe will have a slightly different hop profile, depending on the time of year. It is also not uncommon to see 7venth Sun feature a saison, Berliner weisse, or brettanomyces beer on draft as well. One of the benefits of being a small brewery is that he is always making beer.

Whether Justin is brewing new beer or preparing for the next big event, 7venth Sun is always in motion. Justin is looking to work his way into expansion and keep up with the demand he has, which is a compliment to the caliber of beer that he makes. 7venth Sun also has a great relationship with its neighbors, brewing a collaboration beer with the neighboring Dunedin Brewery within the first months of being open. While 7venth Sun's beer is on draft at many establishments throughout Tampa and some in other parts of Florida, 7venth Sun's creative talent is best sampled through the home taps off Broadway in Dunedin.

Insider Tip: 7venth Sun taps a new beer from its barrel program every Wednesday.

Lagerhaus Brewery

Brewpub
3438 East Lake Road South, Palm Harbor 34685
(727) 216-9682
http://lagerhausbrewery.com
Open 7 days a week

Lagerhaus is a German-themed restaurant that appreciates beer, Bavaria, and beyond. The small brewhouse overlooks the restaurant in the bustling East Lake area of Pinellas County. Brewer Franz Rothschadl Jr. has a history of making great beers, and the goal of the restaurant is to focus on a place where people of all ages can come and enjoy a great beer and some good food in a positive environment. To this end, in summer 2012 Lagerhaus opened up a pet-friendly German-style biergarten outside the restaurant.

Rothschadl has won numerous accolades in brewing over the term of his brewing career. He and a partner opened Lagerhaus after a career working for Hoppers Grill and Brewery (not to be confused with Hops Restaurant) for four years. His Royal Bohemian Pilsner won a gold medal at the Great American Beer Festival in 1999, and he has focused his brewing on German, Belgian, and English beers since opening Lagerhaus. Lagerhaus is another feather in Franz's cap, after opening up several successful brewpubs in Austria and South America, he opened Lagerhaus to help serve great beer to the community where he lives.

Lagerhaus intermixes house beers with draft offerings from macro- and microbreweries alike. Franz also offers members of his

loyalty program, or Lagerhausers, sneak peeks at upcoming beers and advance notice on any events the brewer has on the horizon. The best way to know what the future holds for the taps and the restaurant is to check the website or Facebook page, or better yet to come in for a pint.

The German-style biergarten model that Lagerhaus has adopted allows for food, fresh air, fresh beer, and conversation to be on tap at any time. In an area that keeps moving, Lagerhaus reminds patrons to slow down a minute, even if it's only for a beer and a bratwurst.

Insider's Tip: It is worth the occasional e-mail to sign up for Lagerhaus's loyalty e-mails, the Lagerhausers. Lagerhaus hosts frequent glassware giveaways and special tappings and the loyalty program gives a few days' notice.

Saint Somewhere Brewery

Brewery
1441 Savannah Ave., Unit E, Tarpon Springs 34689
(813) 503-6181
http://saintsomewherebrewing.com
Tours and tastings offered Thursday and Friday evenings, $10 per person (includes three fills of Saint Somewhere beer)

Saint Somewhere Brewery is off the beaten path right on the Pasco/Pinellas County line. The brewery itself is located in an industrial plaza and does not have a set area for a tasting room, but that does not deter Saint Somewhere's owner and head brewer, Bob Sylvester, from hosting tours and tastings on Thursday and Friday nights.

Visiting this brewery is an experience with beers unlike any others in the Tampa Bay area.

Bob Sylvester began Saint Somewhere as a side business, brewing as an escape from his day job. Once the brewery grew in sales, he was able to resign his day job in the retail world and become a full-time brewer, thus realizing every home brewer's dream. Bob has a commitment to making one kind of beer: a Belgian-style farmhouse ale. After brewing his beer with hand-chosen ingredients, he then takes these farmhouse ales a step further and inoculates them with *Brettanomyces* (a type of wild yeast). They are fermented in open containers so the yeasts in the Tarpon Springs breeze can come in and help ferment the beer. As a final step, Sylvester adds extra yeast to the beer upon bottling so the beer will continue to ferment in the bottle. These rustic ales are then bottled by a dedicated group of brewery volunteers and shipped to thirty-four states around the country. To add another layer of Floridiana to the beers, all of the bottle artwork Saint Somewhere uses is from vintage Florida tourist marketing materials.

Saint Somewhere has three core beers that it makes year-round, and several draft offerings that it cycles through periodically as pseudoseasonal offerings. The year round beers are Saison Athene, a saison made with chamomile, rosemary, and black pepper; Lectio Divina, a cross between an abbey dubbel and a saison; and Pays du Soleil, a saison made with palmetto berries and whole hibiscus flowers. Saint Somewhere will also make casks, one-of-a-kind beers for festivals, and random one-off beers to celebrate the unique nature of the beer industry.

Saint Somewhere is a markedly Florida brewery. In almost any other state, brewing a beer utilizing open fermentation would not be feasible for several months out of the year, and few brewers are as open as Bob Sylvester to using wild yeast. Saint Somewhere is a great spot to visit for beer and conversation with Bob and his loyal team of bottlers.

Insider Tip: Since Saint Somewhere's beers are bottle-conditioned and evolve in the bottle, beer tasted fresh at the brewery will be (to the sensitive taster) a bit different from beer in the bottle.

Two Henrys Brewing Company

Brewery
5210 West Thonotosassa Road, Plant City 33565
(813) 752-9100
http://www.twohenrysbrewing.com
Open 7 days a week

Two Henrys Brewing Company is the result of a melding of the minds of winemakers who realized that they had lots of land and many ideas of how to entice additional patrons to their tasting room. The brewery and tasting room is housed on the twenty-five acres owned by the Keel and Curely Winery, a fixture in Tampa and Plant City viticulture. The brewery combines modern and traditional beer styles and aims to stay fairly local, at least while the brewery goes through adolescence.

Two Henrys Brewing Company is named for Henry Plant and Henry Flagler, two men who had the foresight to see past the messes of post–Civil War Florida and infuse enough capital to transform Florida by building railroads and bringing tourists to the state's sunny shores. The brewery opened its doors on October 19, 2013, and plans to mark that occasion every year with a Biertoberfest. The brewery does not have plans to conquer the world, but on its seven-barrel brewing system, it simply aims to make great, local, accessible beer.

The locomotive of the Two Henrys train is a 7-percent alcohol dark IPA known as The Eighth Wonder. Owner Clay Keel describes the beer as a "Simcoe-heavy." For opening day, the brewery had batches of stouts, pale ale, IPA, brown ale, and lagers. Two Henrys' recipe book has several entries that will come to fruition as the brewery progresses.

Insider Tip: Two Henrys Brewing shares grounds with Keel and Curley Winery. Bring a wine lover, and he or she can try a sample for $6. Also note that Two Henrys only fills growlers from its brewery.

Southern Brewing and Winemaking

Brewery
4500 North Nebraska Ave., Tampa 33603
(813) 238-7800
http://southernbrewingwinemaking.com
Closed Monday

Southern Brewing and Winemaking are the experts that carry the supplies for home brewers and home vintners to make their wares. They also help self-made zymurgists troubleshoot any issues with brewing or winemaking, so it only made sense that they would start a brewery to illustrate the endless possibilities of brewing.

The brewery and retail shop are the brainchild of owners, Brian and Kelly Fenstermacher. Brian was the manager and brewer at the Ybor City Brewing Company, which was one of the earliest craft breweries to try to revive craft beer in the Tampa area. Brian has also distributed grain and opened Southern Brewing and Winemaking in 2008 as a wholesale warehouse. The company eventually shifted its focus to home brewing supply and in January 2012 moved into their current space and added a one-barrel brewing system and a tap room to enjoy the fruits of their labor. The store was already staffed with brewers, and now they had twenty-four taps to fill with anything their hearts desired to brew. Because the store already carried 110 different grains, fifty different types of hops, and a plentiful number of yeasts, the brewers were set free to brew small batches of infinite possibilities. One other noteworthy item

about Southern Brewing is that the owners have almost no desire to distribute their beers offsite, so sampling them requires a trip to the brewery.

The brewery quickly got to work on filling the taps, and the tap room has a few beers that cycle through regularly with about ten core beers that are usually in the mix of taps; the rest of the taps are either guest taps or products of the brewer's imagination. Brian is a fan of IPAs, so he tries to keep at least three on at all times. Rick, one of the other brewers, is a fan of Belgian beers, so there are usually several Belgian-inspired beers on as well. The other taps are anything from an apple mead to a deep obsidian-colored imperial stout to a light Berliner weisse to a Flanders-style sour red ale.

The brewers at Southern Brewing and Winemaking are living a home brewer's dream: they have a brewing system that allows them to cycle through whatever creation they can dream of producing and then serve that beer, mead, or cider to the public and continue to make more of the beers they like. Brian says that every brewer in the house approaches recipe creation differently, so each beer is a reflection of the synthesis of imagination and ingredients, but only in one-barrel increments.

Florida Avenue Brewing Company (formerly Cold Storage Craft Brewery)

Brewery
4101 North Florida Ave., Tampa 33603
(813) 374-2101
http://floridaavenuebrewing.com
Closed Sunday and Monday

Florida Avenue Brewing Co. came quietly into the Tampa brewing market and moved swiftly to get its beers into numerous outlets around town. Before the tasting room opened for patrons,

the brewery was open to the public only one day each month for tours and tastings. The brewery christened itself as Cold Storage Craft Brewery after the Cold Storage Café in downtown Tampa but quickly saw that the public had an affinity for its "Florida Avenue Ales," so the brewery renamed itself Florida Avenue Brewing Co.

The brewery began in July of 2010 when a veteran home brewer and his business partners found a defunct grocery store. The warehouse was sitting vacant, so the partners renovated the building, added a business room where distributors and business associates could meet to sample the brewery's beers, and went in search of brewing equipment. In the brewing industry today, there are usually many breweries in the early stages of establishment so used brewing equipment of good quality is sold very quickly, and new brewing equipment can take several weeks to several months to fabricate. The owners were prepared for a long search. Yet fortune seemed to favor Florida Avenue Brewing, and the brewing equipment from the Anheuser-Busch Tampa brewery at Busch Gardens had been sitting vacant at the park property and was sold in the wake of the AB-InBev merger. Florida Avenue Brewing was able to acquire some of Tampa's most historic brewing vessels for its maiden voyage on the sea of craft beer.

Florida Avenue Brewing Co. takes pride in the quality and consistency of its beer. The brewery pours three core beers into six-packs: Florida Avenue Ale, Florida Avenue Blueberry Ale, and Florida Avenue India Pale Ale. The brewery also cycles into seasonal beers, with an amber ale dubbed Copperhead Ale and a brown ale dubbed Betchy Brown. Florida Avenue is available on draft from Saint Petersburg to Tampa to Orlando, south to Key West, and north to Gainesville and Saint Augustine.

Florida Avenue Brewing Co. brews consistent, traditional, smooth core beers and should begin to work on more experimental and limited brews once it completes a round of expansion.

Big Storm Brewery

Brewery
2438 Merchant Ave., #103, Odessa, 33556
(727) 807-7998
http://bigstormbrewery.com
Open 7 days a week

Begun by two friends, Big Storm is a small brewery in Odessa is Pasco County's first (and currently only) microbrewery. The brewery's tasting room opened in September of 2012, and the brewery and its beers are picking up in intensity.

Clay Yarn and Mike Bishop, two alumni from the University of South Florida, were working by day and getting together to share beers at night. They decided that there existed a perfect storm of

conditions in their lives and so they put together a business plan to start a brewery. Once the business plan was assembled, capital was gathered, and the location secured for Odessa, a launch date of Friday, July 13, 2012, was set. From that point forward, the storm has been raging on; the brewery was built with expansion in mind, as pipes were plumbed for future expansion at the time of construction and the space was selected for its height, so larger fermenters would fall into place.

The beer that built Big Storm is an amber ale, dubbed Wavemaker Amber Ale. Wavemaker is a bit of a malt bomb, and at 5.6 percent alcohol, this beer may make waves but does not grab with the undertow. As a brewer, Bishop is working through recipes. Starting in 2012, Big Storm has made its signature amber ale, a sweet IPA, dubbed Arcus IPA, and a smoked rye beer, dubbed Brushfire Rye Ale. Palm Bender Pale Ale and a rye beer called Ryse and Shine made their debut in 2013. The brewery's oatmeal stout, Oats in Hose, was aged in a bourbon barrel for its release in early summer. Next Big Storm expanded its 3.5-barrel brewing system to a 15-barrel brewing system. Translation: more beer is on the way.

While Big Storm Brewery started small, it is picking up steam around Tampa. Its beer has won accolades from the Best Florida Beer Competition, and brewer Mike Bishop won a scholarship to the Siebel Institute of Brewing from the Florida Brewers' Guild based on the merits of his beer. With a small tasting room adjacent to the brewery and growing interest in one of Tampa's youngest craft breweries, there will be many more storms issuing forth from the Odessa brewery.

Three Palms Brewing

Brewery
1509 Hobbs St., Tampa 33619
(888) 813-4859
http://threepalmsbrewing.com
Closed Monday and Tuesday

Three Palms Brewing is one of Tampa's smaller breweries nestled into the Brandon area. Off beaten path, a left, another left, and down the dirt road, the tap room is open and the beer is flowing.

Former contractor and brewer Randy Reaver founded Three Palms Brewing when he was laid off from his previous job as a network engineer. Reaver home brewed for five years before deciding to open a brewery of his own. Of course, the eleven-brewery tour of Denver helped persuade him to take a leap of faith. Three Palms is currently housed in an industrial park in Brandon and was born on the fourth of July in 2012; at least that's when the first batch of Three Palms beer was made after all the planning and permitting was done for the brewery.

Currently Reaver is working to fill his kegs as quickly as one man can. Three Palms offers three mainstays: one is a hoppy red called Ruby Pogo, one is a citrusy IPA called Pindo, and the third is the first beer offered by Three Palms, Queen of Wheat Hefeweizen. Three Palms also has ambitions of packaging beer in cans in the near future, as well as possibly beginning to age beer in spirit barrels. While Randy expands his repertoire into offering a barley wine, chocolate stout, and Berliner weisse, those beers are offered in limited capacity and head straight to the tasting room. The Three Palms tasting room is the direct pipeline to the source and usually contains exclusive beers.

Three Palms is one of Tampa's smaller breweries, but in craft beer it is beer quality, not brewery size, that dictates consumer opinion.

Three Palms continues to brew beer for its consumers' and employees' likes and would prefer to let growth take its course naturally.

Barley Mow Brewing Company

Brewery
518 West Bay Dr., Largo 33770
(727) 584-7772
http://barleymowbrewingco.com
Open 7 days a week

Barley Mow Brewing Company is the city of Largo's only craft brewery and began its existence as a craft beer bar in November of 2011. Experienced brewer and owner Jay Dingman had wanted to begin brewing at his place, but an elongated permitting process forced Dingman and his wife to put off pouring their first house beer until July of 2012. Like a few other breweries across Florida, Barley Mow uses the smaller size of the brewery as an advantage, rotating taps and adding new house beers often.

Jay Dingman's beer education (and the roots of Barley Mow) began in Longmont, Colorado, when his roommate began working for Left Hand Brewing Company. As Jay learned more about beer, he wanted to open his own brewery. When he met his wife and found out that she was also into craft beer, the idea for Barley Mow Brewing Company was conceived. The new brewery owners transformed the remnants of an old, dark wooden Irish pub on the main thoroughfare of Bay Drive in Largo. They kept the darker wood, and added a small two-barrel brew house to the pub, sharing space with the bar. The brewery and tasting room essentially exist in the same space and is currently staffed by six people, including the Dingmans, who both brew and tend bar.

Barley Mow is named for a fourteenth-century Gaelic ode to the barley harvest, and the brewery certainly celebrates its fruits. Look

for many rotating taps as Barley Mow works to keep up with demand and a few mainstays on the list. As the beers turn over, sometimes an old favorite rotates out, but some beers cycle back on tap faster than others, like bestselling and very citrus-forward Quackalope IPA, named for a statue overlooking the bar, and a black IPA named The Unkindness, after the traditional name for a flock of ravens. Aside from those, look for the taps to pour anything from a marshmallow stout to a California Common Beer to a light and fruity blonde ale. Of fourteen taps, almost all bear house beer, and the others are guest taps.

Barley Mow Brewing Company is only nine miles from Dunedin and a short drive from most other places in Tampa, but with Tampa traffic, it becomes a destination location. If drinking beer does not satisfy the curious, then Barley Mow sponsors days for patrons to learn how to brew beer, including occasional seminars on the topic. While Barley Mow hopes to open a separate facility to produce its beer in the future, for now only the brewery and a few accounts around Pinellas County pour Barley Mow's libations.

Sarasota Brewing Company

Brewpub
6607 Gateway Ave., Sarasota 34231
(941) 925-2337
http://sarasotabrewing.com
Open 7 days a week

Sarasota Brewing Co. is a small sports bar turned brewpub with many house beers on tap with beer from other micro- and macro-breweries around the country. Dark wood welcomes patrons into the bar area and the adjoining restaurant, as this neighborhood hangout serves a frosty pint and has several TVs around to show any sporting events of interest.

Vince Pelosi, the brewer, came on board with Sarasota Brewing about six years ago and has worked to make its beers represent a wide variety of beer styles. Many of the light lagers will pair well with sporting events as the light body and relatively low alcohol volume will allow for several beers over the course of a football, baseball, or basketball game.

Sarasota's lineup involves a healthy mix of ales and lagers with several seasonal rotations included. While Sarasota Brewing makes lighter lagers and some hoppy ambers, Vince still has room to be creative. Vince also works out his brewing muscles as he occasionally puts on different and one-off beers like a Belgian quadruple made with rosemary or other such tasty offerings.

Sarasota Brewing has been pouring in Sarasota's Gulfgate neighborhood since before the craft beer revolution and has the stuff to maintain for a while. With several craft beer bars in the area and new craft breweries opening in Sarasota, Sarasota Brewing is helping to make Sarasota a beer destination.

Darwin's on 4th

Brewpub
1525 4th St., Sarasota 34236
(941) 343-2165
http://darwinson4th.com
Closed Sunday

Darwin's on 4th has quickly evolved into a fixture of Sarasota's craft beer movement, and the fittest brews survive into the main lineup of this Peruvian gastro brewpub. An earthy yet relaxed atmosphere greets diners as dinner is being prepared (currently Darwin's is only open for dinner). Chef and owner Darwin Santa Maria has a keen eye for the food that leaves his kitchen and brewmaster Jorge Rosabal does the same in the brewhouse, with a weather eye on the beer horizon.

One of the superstitions of owning a restaurant or brewery is that building a future business on the spot of a failed business is a significant challenge. Darwin's on 4th has proven that this superstition does not apply here, as the restaurant was built on the bones of the old Mad Crow restaurant, which went out of business months before Darwin's renovated the space and imbued the ambiance, spirit, and artistry of Peru into the place. With that newly instilled style comes cuisine and beers meant to evoke the flavors of Peru and South America. Jorge seeks to produce beers that will complement the kitchen's artistry and to this end, every beer on the bar menu is listed with an ideal dish that pairs with it. Brewmaster Jorge has brewed in large breweries in Honduras, which gave him the expertise to land the job at Darwin's, and he will soon oversee the Darwin's production facility in Bradenton in addition to the restaurant in Sarasota.

The restaurant brewpub began with a small brewing system, yet recent expansion will grow the availability of Darwin's beers in the pub. Other beers rotating on draft include a saison made with lemongrass, a West Coast style IPA called Summadayze (which was voted the second-best beer in Florida at the 2013 Best Florida Beer Competition), and Quinoa Cerveza, made from the quinoa grain. Whatever the occasion or the twist, Rosabal works to keep the taps flowing with his beers for the thirsty dinner crowd.

Darwin's is the only Peruvian food and brewpub in the state of Florida. With this unique amalgamation of food and beer goes hand in hand with just the type of distinctive experience that craft beer is trying to create throughout the United States. Darwin's on 4th showcases the heights of ethnic cuisine and the versatility of flavors in that cuisine's liquid company.

Zeke's Brewing

Brewery
333 North Falkenburg Road, Unit D-408, Tampa 33619
(813) 410-5438
http://www.zekesbrew.com
Hours not set. Call ahead.

While Zeke's story is another one of a home brewer turned professional, the surprise ending comes with how long Zeke's brewer Zac Myers has been brewing—one year. Myers knew after brewing his first batch of all-grain home brew that he wanted to join the ranks of professional brewers and open his own brewery. Less than a year later, July 2013, Zeke's Brewing opened in the Brandon area of Tampa.

To say that Zeke's is a labor of love is an understatement: virtually everything in the brewery was built or fitted by Myers, from the bar and cooling unit that he worked on to the mash tun that traveled 2,700 miles to Zeke's. Myers works an all-day sales job then works at the brewery until 10 p.m., taking care of all the brewery's operations and then starting the process over.

While Zeke's beers are rotating based on demand, Myers tries to keep five beers rotating as his core beers. Zeke's has the English-style Ale, with its tones of chocolate and toffee; the American Pale Ale, hopped with five different hops; the clean and full-bodied Red Betty Ale; the Harbor View IPA with six different hops, finishing at 6.5 percent alcohol; and finally the Lazy Lager with the clean finish of a pilsner with 6.5 percent alcohol. As for seasonals, Zac plans to rotate an Oktoberfest in the fall, a Belgian "Straw Blonde" Berry Ale, and a Scottish ale, The Bog, in the winter.

Zeke's is the second brewery to open doors in the Brandon area—look for expansion and new ideas from this small brewery.

R Bar Brewing Company

Brewpub
245 108th Avenue, Treasure Island 33706
(727) 367-3400
http://rbarti.com
Open 7 days a week

R Bar Brewing Company is the first craft brewery among the beaches in Pinellas County.

R Bar is located in a building that housed an A&W Root Beer stand in its past life. When Bob Hughes bought the bar in December of 2011, he began renovating the space and making small improvements that would help the bar stand out in the Treasure Island area. One item that immediately stood out to Hughes was the idea that he had a cook who knew how to make beer. Fast forward three months, dollars spent for a brewpub license, and the experience of a thirteen-year home brewer in the brewhouse, and R Bar Brewing Company was born.

R Bar brews on a ten-gallon brewing system in the crowded kitchen with brewer Eric Richardson at the helm. While R Bar is having trouble keeping up with the demand, part of the problem is a lack of room to expand. Treasure Island cycles through many tourists, and when everyone is interested in house beers, it makes for a diminished supply.

Eric has brewed numerous different beers on the system at R Bar, the beauty of limited size is the ability to turn over beer quickly, given ample time for fermentation. He makes a porter that he tries to keep on tap regularly, followed by a blonde ale, and several different versions of pale ales and IPAs. The brewery also makes a pumpkin ale once the weather starts to turn and a coconut IPA for the adventurous.

R Bar's beers are only available on draft at the Treasure Island pub, and even then are at the mercy of thirsty locals.

3 Daughters Brewing

Brewery
222 22nd Street South, Saint Petersburg 33712
(727) 495-6002
http://www.3dbrewing.com
Closed Sunday

With 150 years' of brewing in the family, 3 Daughters Brewing is reminding people to enjoy the moments with good beer and good friends.

3 Daughters Brewing is owned by Mike Harting, one of the co-owners of the bistro Bella Brava. Mike met Ty Weaver in the kitchen at Bella Brava. Mike and Ty first came up with the idea of brewing beer when Mike wanted house beer for beer-battered fish. The idea then grew from fish batter into house beers at Bella Brava, then Weaver's beers grew so popular that they could be the bar's best sellers on any given weekend. Then, Mike thought, what if we built a production brewery? Weaver's latest challenge has him concocting beers for 3 Daughters at a massive warehouse production brewery that is yet another star in Saint Petersburg's illustrious skyline.

Brewing its beers on a thirty-barrel brewing system in their Saint Petersburg production facility and tasting room, 3 Daughters' core beers show off the drinkability of sessionable beers with flavors of special occasion sipping beers, starting with Beach Blonde Ale, the 5 percent light-colored beer that pairs well with a skyrocketing thermometer. Brown Pelican, a Dunkelweizen, or dark German wheat beer, which is full of banana and clove yeasty aroma but under 6 percent alcohol. Finally, the smooth-bodied, sessionable Summer Storm Oatmeal Stout rounds out the lineup bringing 5.2 percent alcohol and flavors of coffee and chocolate to the table.

3 Daughters Brewing's beer is available in the Tampa Bay area and will expand organically from its Saint Petersburg home.

Insider Tip: Harting and company also plan to have a quality lab onsite where home brewers can make appointments and bring their beers in to be analyzed.

St. Pete Brewing Company

Brewery
544 First Avenue North, Saint Petersburg 33701
(727) 692-8809
http://www.stpetebrew.com
Closed Monday

St. Pete Brewing Company is an old name of beer with a new face in 2013. The brewery is the brainchild of brewer Tom Williams, who thought it would be ideal to get St. Pete Brewing's beers to market before building the brewery. St. Pete Orange Wheat and Pinellas Pale Ale were brought to their namesake areas and beyond into the thirsty Tampa market via contract brewing before the brewery was even approved for construction.

St. Pete Brewing operates a ten-barrel brewing system and, with the help of tanks purchased from Big Storm Brewing in Odessa, began operations on equipment with a history. St. Pete Brewing's brewer, Jon McCracken, comes to the brewery by way of Vermont and California with brewing experience to match and an eye toward traditional brews.

St. Pete Brewing brews beers for the endless Florida summer. While Pinellas Pale Ale and St. Pete Orange Wheat remain core beers at St. Pete Brewing Company, no brewery in Florida seems complete without an IPA to call its own.

Look for St. Pete Brewing's beers throughout Pinellas and Hillsborough Counties, and as growth begins, so should expansion.

Brewers' Tasting Room

Brewpub
11270 4th Street North, Suite 202, Saint Petersburg 33716
(727) 873-3900
http://www.brewerstastingroom.com
Closed Monday

Brewers' Tasting Room is one of those establishments that blurs the line between brewer and home brewer, but owner Rick Wolfe is community-minded and full of passion when it comes to craft beer making, so it is impossible not to include Brewers' Tasting Room in a list of Tampa-area breweries.

Brewers' Tasting Room is a launching point for quality beer. The idea behind Brewers' Tasting Room is to find the best brewers from home brewers to commercial brewers and allow them to come in and work with Brewers' Tasting Room staff. Brewers first create a beer, brew it on BTR's brewing system, and after it is ready, to serve it in the tasting room while tracking the beer's popularity in order to give a brewer a genuine picture of how his or her beer is received.

To be clear, not everyone is cut out to brew on the system at Brewers' Tasting Room. For home brewers, it is possible to submit home brew for judging, and the staff along with Beer Judge Certification Program certified beer judges will evaluate the beer. If the beer makes the grade, then Wolfe will pay for the ingredients and arrange to brew the beer on his two-barrel system in exchange for the right to pour the beer from BTR's taps.

There are no core beers from Brewers' Tasting Room, as the rest of the taps are filled in by commercial beer from around the United States, with a focus on local beer.

Saint Somewhere's Bob Sylvester, Doug Dozark from Cycle Brewing, and J. Wakefield Brewing's Johnathan Wakefield have already brewed beers on Wolfe's brewing system. Home brewers and future commercial brewers like Late Start Brewery have also contributed their beers to BTR's tap list. The selection at BTR is based on what the community of brewers in the Tampa area or the state of Florida have brought forth at Brewers' Tasting Room on any given night.

Big Top Brewing Company

Brewery
6111 Porter Way, Sarasota 34232
(800) 590-2448
http://www.bigtopbrewing.com
Open 7 days a week

Another member of Sarasota's Class of 2013, Big Top Brewing Company is the vision of several individuals, including brewer Josh Wilson and CEO Mike Bishaha, reflecting on Sarasota's history as the winter home of the Ringling Circus.

Big Top Brewing Company opened with a mission to brew great beer and helped to bookmark Sarasota as a location with great beer. Plenty of that beer will come from brewing on Big Top's thirty-barrel brewing system and 150 barrels of fermentation capacity. The brewery has three core beers, drawing inspiration from Sarasota and the local community for names: Suncoast Pale Ale, Circus City IPA, and Trapeze Monk Belgian Wit. The brewery has a pilot system, which will allow it the flexibility to try out new beers on the market before brewing anything on a large commercial scale. Finally, Big Top has plans to work on ales, saisons, and sour beers with ideas for barrel-aged beers as the circus train keeps rolling.

Big Top's beers are available in Hillsborough, Pasco, Sarasota, Manatee, and Collier Counties.

Copp Winery and Brewery

Brewery
11 Northeast 4th Avenue, Crystal River 34429
(352) 564-9463
http://www.coppbrewery.com
Closed Monday and Tuesday

Copp Winery and Brewery is Citrus County's craft brewery. The brewery is located off US 98 in Crystal River, and is Florida's northernmost combination winery/brewery. With its welcoming atmosphere, wooden interior, and Napa-comes-to-Florida facility, Copp brewery is a destination brewery for a beer enthusiast and his or her wine-loving family.

The Copp Winery and Brewery is owned by a husband and wife team: Fran and Donna Copp. Fran brews the beers and Donna crafts the wines. Copp Winery and Brewery originally opened as only Copp Winery. Donna began making wines, and seven years later they decided to progress into brewing beers onsite in a one-barrel brewing system with fermenters that hold two barrels of beer. This means that in order to fully fill a fermenter, Fran had to brew two batches of beer. Copp was up to about sixty batches in 2013, and around that same time the couple upgraded the brewer's licensure with the state of Florida to a full brewery license. One of the immediate changes when upgrading was the ability to fill 32 oz growlers. While the brewery is looking at expanding its tap list and upgrading its brew system, most of the beer will remain in-house.

Copp Brewery is working to rotate taps and add new beers all the time with a lineup of several core beers that allow beer-loving locals the opportunity to keep enjoying their favorites. The core beers offered are True Grit, a light-colored pale ale brewed with yellow corn grits to add a bit of sweetness and a light mouthfeel; Hoppy Copp, a 6 percent citrusy IPA with a crisp finish; Center Field Brown, a 4.2 percent brown ale with hints of toasted malts and some citrus hops; and Double Black Stout, a 6 percent stout with notes of chocolate and espresso. After the regulars, the seasonals and limited taps may include anything from a Belgian rye ale to a minty stout to a rum-barrel-aged Jamaican imperial stout.

While Citrus County's locals have already discovered Copp Winery and Brewery, the word is also getting out in the beer community at large. For many around Florida, Crystal River's brewery is a destination brewery, but while travel is required, the effort is worth the rewards: ten taps of fresh craft beer, brewed onsite, and comfortable environs in which to enjoy it.

Cigar City Airport Pub

Brewpub
Airside C, 4100 George J. Bean Parkway, Tampa 33607
(813) 870-8700
http://www.CigarCityBrewing.com
Open 7 days a week

Upon walking up to the Cigar City Airport Pub, you could easily think that the airport has simply transplanted a piece of Ybor City into the concourse. The pub stands, bricks and all, as a substitute for those who cannot make the trek to Ybor City (or the brewery that is infamously not in Ybor) and serves Cigar City's core lineup, seasonals, and a brew or two made onsite at the airport pub.

The tiny pub opened in May of 2012 and is one of the only airport pubs in the world that actually brews beer in the airport. The airport pub pours Tony Jannus Pale Ale, a hoppy treat named for one of the first commercial aviators who ran flights between Tampa and Saint Petersburg, and also boasts several exclusive and elusive beers like Sikorsky Red Ale, Mile High Ale, and Overhead Bin Brown Ale.

The simple pub offers travelers a haven during a layover or a last pint before a departing flight. This little pub does not substitute for a visit to Tampa's production brewery; it simply offers fliers a taste of Tampa before takeoff.

Angry Chair Brewing

Brewery
6401 North Florida Avenue, Tampa 33604
(813) 892-1651
http://angrychairbrewing.com
Call for hours

Angry Chair Brewing is the little brewery in Seminole Heights that makes a lot of crazy beer. How crazy? If the beers they have poured at Tampa Area Festivals are any indication, then it will be everything from a low-alcohol Berliner weisse to a high gravity barrel-aged treat.

Brewer Ben Romano made a name for himself as Cigar City Brewing's pilot brewer. In striking out on his own with Angry Chair as his production brewery, Ben has made standout beers, like his Flambe Strong Ale, numerous Florida weisses, and sour ales, which have earned the brewery accolades from scores of beer fans at Tampa Bay Beer Week's Halfway There Festival.

While Angry Chair has the beers that will make the perfect company to any dish, Angry Chair also makes beers that will substitute for any dish, including dessert. Angry Chair once hosted a dinner at the Cigar City Brewpub where all of its beers were dessert beers, each one more decadent than the previous, with the final course being Coconut Banana Cream Pie Ale aged in a bourbon barrel. Ben Romano around brewing equipment is like Mr. Scott in the engine room. Great things are to be expected as Angry Chair continues to develop.

Six Ten Brewing Company

Brewery
7052 Benjamin Road, Tampa 33634
(813) 886-0610
http://www.sixtenbrewing.com
Closed Monday and Tuesday

Six Ten Brewing Company is another award-winning home brewer pushing to begin making his beer available to the local market. Six Ten Brewing welcomed 2014 as the year that Chris and Leslie Johnson quit their nine-to-five jobs and began living their lives for their six-to-ten.

Six Ten stands as a salute to that dream job that many folks work when away from the nine-to-five grind. For years, Chris and Leslie Johnson worked in information technology and brewed at night and on weekends. Chris has brewed for twenty years, and his beers have won awards in local, state, and national competitions. Six Ten opened with a ten-barrel brewing system and a small tasting room to host the local community and show off their liquid wares.

Coppertail Brewing Company

Brewery
2601 East Second Avenue, Tampa 33605
(813) 247-1500
http://www.coppertailbrewing.com
Call for hours

Coppertail Brewing combines the talents and passions of home brewers Robb Larson and Kent Bailey. The pair decided to open a craft brewery and named it Coppertail Brewing, after an imaginary monster that Kent's young daughter dreamt up.

When Larson and Bailey got the brewery started in the right direction, in April of 2013, they brought in professional brewer Casey Hughes, formerly of Flying Fish Brewing in New Jersey. Hughes would bring brewing know-how of production brewing that would move Coppertail forward. The brewery features 35,000 square feet of space, including a 2,000-square-foot tasting room. Hughes's master plan is to work on barrel-aging, sour beers, and special releases in addition to working out at least four core beers with rotating seasonals.

The brewery's location is adjacent to the labyrinthine IKEA store in Ybor City and has a history of its own. The brewery once housed a Hellman's mayonnaise factory, the Seville Olive Company, and refrigerated storage. Coppertail has a fifty-barrel brewing system; that's over 1,500 gallons of beer in one batch. Hughes, along with

Larson and Bailey, worked on Coppertail's pilot system to brew beers for festivals and events to promote the brewery before opening. Following in the Florida spirit, Coppertail also collaborated with Khris Johnson of Green Bench Brewing and Oxbow Brewing of Maine to produce beers for thirsty fans before their equipment was even in place.

Ulele Brewpub

Brewpub
1810 North Highland, Tampa 33602
http://www.uleletampa.com
Call for hours

Owned by the Columbia Restaurant Group, Ulele Brewpub features "native-inspired brews." The pub's location is at the head of Ulele Spring, one of the springs that fed Tampa when it was Fort Brooke, now part of Tampa's Water Works Park. Ulele opened in the former Tampa Water Works plant, a Tampa Heights structure built in 1903 that at one point handled three million gallons of water each day.

Under the direction of head brewer Tim Shackton, an alumnus of the Hops brewing chain, the restaurant plans to brew its beers on premises in Ybor City, and serve them directly from the brite tank, putting the freshest possible beer into the glasses of patrons.

ESB Brewing Company

Brewery
333 Falkenburg Road North, Unit D-407, Tampa 33619
(813) 990-0700
http://www.esbbrewing.com
Closed Monday and Tuesday

ESB Brewing is what happens when a home brew store owner has lots of time to think about the kinds of beers he would brew and unites like-minded friends behind this cause. ESB Brewing is Booth Brewing's sister company: production breweries that pair together like cheddar cheese and an IPA.

In 2003, a group of home brewers got together and began speaking about what their ideal breweries would look like. Fast forward a few years when Francis Booth, of Booth Brewing, and friend Bobby Every both decided to open a brewery, they discovered that it was quite the herculean task. The two decided to join forces and open one brewery. The friends discovered that they had a builder and a brewer, but they needed someone to market the place. With the addition of a marketing guy, the three combined their initials and ESB Brewing emerged.

ESB Brewing began brewing in 2013 after obtaining its state license, and from there they opened a tasting room on-site. ESB has a goal of producing about one hundred kegs each week, and currently it is about halfway to that goal. Its beers are distributed through Pasco and Hillsborough, and at any time the brewery has fifteen house beers on tap in its tasting room, including some beers brewed with yeast caught from the air that was captured, cultured, and used in brewing. Like few other breweries, one can literally taste some of the city in ESB's beer.

ESB has chosen to show off the Florida lifestyle with a nod to the pirate roots of Tampa Bay, and it names the beers along those lines. Its core beers, and the ones that will see the widest distribution, are the Pieces of Eight Double IPA, an 8 percent, aggressive and balanced DIPA with eight hops; Gaspar's Agave Wheat, a wheat ale with some added rye to balance the finish and sweetened with an addition of agave syrup, named for pirate Jose Gaspar. ESB also has a number of beers to span the spectrum of beer styles, from Anne Bonny Cherry Chocolate Stout to Pirate Gold Golden Ale, a seasonal Smoked Pumpkin Porter, a Pecan Porter, and Bourbon Barrel Imperial Stout. With so many taps and the resources of a home brew store, the only limit is what the brewer's imagination can fathom.

Insider Tip: ESB is proud to be one of only six breweries in the United States that boast a woman as their head brewer.

The Wild Rover Pub and Brewery

Brewery
8740 North Mobley Road, Odessa 33556
(813) 475-5995
http://thewildroverbrewery.com
Closed Sunday

The Wild Rover Pub and Brewery was born from a desire to bring the heart and feel of a cozy English pub to the Keystone area of Pasco and Pinellas Counties.

Father-and-son team Derek and Ricky Wells founded and built the Wild Rover as a local brewpub, where friends could come socialize and have a beer brewed in their community.

The Wild Rover brews on a four-barrel brewing system and seeks to combine the communal feel of an English pub with the aggressive beers of American craft beer.

With the feel of a traditional English pub come many traditional English styles, except with the admission that this is not England, so a few beer style additions were necessary. The Wild Rover's beers run through the spectrum of styles from an English mild dubbed the Mild Rover to Sister Golden Ale to the behemoth of John Barleywine Must Die.

JDub's Brewing Company

Brewery
1215 Mango Avenue, Sarasota 34237
(941) 955-2739
http://www.jdubsbrewing.com
Closed Monday through Wednesday

JDub's Brewing Company is what happens when the seeds of a dream take root in the Florida soil. Brewery owner Jeremy Joerger took a leap of faith, left a lucrative government job in Washington, D.C., and moved down to Sarasota to build a craft brewery in which Sarasota could take pride.

That dream led Jeremy to open JDub's Brewing Company—a brewery that strives to brew quality beers as creative as its namesake. The brewery will brew fifteen barrels at a time for its core beers: Up Top! IPA, an authentic German Pilsner called Yodeler Pils, and a third, yet-to-be-determined core beer. In the spirit of quality and creativity, JDub's will also feature a three-barrel pilot system, so that the community can try out ideas for new beers and give feedback directly to the brewery.

JDub's began construction in October 2013 and opened in February 2014. While Joerger watches over the business side of things, the brewhouse is the purview of Tom Harris, former brewer of Long Trail Brewing Company in Vermont (the eighteenth-largest craft brewer in the United States). Tom began to materialize his vision for JDub's from the moment he moved to Florida and hopes to continue that vision as he creates a barrel aging program and sour program at JDub's.

A1A Ale Works offerings, Saint Augustine

Above: Brewzzi kettle, Boca Raton

Right: Darwin's on 4th exterior, Sarasota

Cask and Larder brewing system, Orlando

DeSoto Beer poster, Tampa

The Funky Buddha Lounge and Brewery interior, Boca Raton

Silver Bar Beer poster, Tampa

Hourglass Brewery system, Orlando

Left: Peg's Cantina exterior

Below: Mile Marker Brewing system, Saint Augustine

Rapp Brewing tap room, Seminole

Swamp Head Brewery, Gainesville

Motorworks Brewing Company

Brewery
1014 Ninth Street West, Bradenton 34205
(941) 567-6218
http://www.motorworksbrewing.com
Open 7 days a week

Motorworks Brewing Company is the result of Frank and Denise Tschida's desire to root their business in downtown Bradenton. Their plan to utilize 23,000 square feet of brewing space in a building that previously held a Chevrolet, Chrysler, and Hudson Motors dealership gives the brewery its name. The brewery began construction in July 2013 to renovate the former car dealership into a brewery, tap room, and biergarten.

All Motorworks beers are crafted by head brewer Bob Haa either on the three-and-a-half-barrel pilot system or on the thirty-barrel commercial brewing system. Haa is an alumnus of the Hops chain of breweries, where he was a research and development brewer.

Darwin Brewing Company

Brewery
803 Seventeenth Avenue West, Bradenton 34205
(941) 747-1970
http://www.darwinbrewingco.com
Closed Monday

From the same team that brought beer to Darwin's on 4th comes a production brewery in Bradenton. Darwin's production facility features beers crafted by brewer Jorge Rosabal in a larger setting. This production facility allows Rosabal the space and a fifteen-barrel brewing system to package his beers for shipment into distribution, as opposed to the brewpub in Sarasota, whose seven-barrel brewing system was optimized to make beer for the restaurant. Distribution is set to begin in an initial burst into Sarasota and Manatee Counties while ready for growth beyond.

Darwin Brewing Company's production facility will be home to core beers that will be initially kegged and soon after canned. The year-round beers of the production facility will be Circa 1926, a tangerine wheat beer; Ayawasca, a Belgian strong ale; the award-winning Sumadayze IPA; and the easy-drinking Pirata Pilsner. As always, the freshest beer will be poured from the source, and the tasting room will be home to limited beers and exclusive treatments.

Darwin Brewing Company began with a kitchen and a taste for good beer, and expanded outward to give Sarasota the answer for its thirst questions.

BREWERIES IN FERMENTATION

While many other areas around the state are still giving birth to the idea of handcrafted beer, Tampa has always been the epicenter—both of nineteenth-century and twenty-first-century Florida craft beer. Tampa's breweries have brewed uncompromisingly and relentlessly to achieve their current level of success and the next generation of brewers is ready to take up the torch. Below are a few of Tampa's future craft breweries and their statuses.

Little Giant Brewery

Owner and brewer Michael Wagner has had to endure repeated setbacks in pursuit of his dream to open a brewery in the Sarasota/Bradenton area. Wagner has been a fixture at festivals and special events and has been featured on the cover of *Beer Advocate* magazine as an up-and-coming Florida brewer. Each time Wagner would settle on a place, he would have to move or need a change. With the move to the facility on 7th Street in Bradenton, Wagner's troubles seemed to subside, and there he found the rock upon which to build his brewery.

Michael Wagner is an alumnus of Wabash College, whose mascots were the little giants. Once he became a brewer, Wagner thought the name of his college mascots would be an appropriate moniker for his brewery, so Little Giant Brewery was born. Little Giant currently has an old event space that he is using to make beer, and this space will evolve and transform to become the Little Giant Tasting Room. Wagner will be using twenty- and forty-barrel fermenters in a 5,500-square-foot warehouse to make and sustain Little Giant's beers. The brewery will have an adjacent tasting room to serve its wares once it is fully operational.

Wagner describes Little Giant's beers as balanced, traditional, quaffable, high-quality love in a glass. Once the brewery is operational, he hopes to have a porter, pale ale, IPA, and alt as his core beers. Wagner also hopes to rotate through almost every style of beer in his quest to find just the right seasonals and work up to a modest barrel program in the brewery's first years. All of this will be possible in the space he has, plus additional room for more tank space.

Little Giant is slated to open, with a small production facility and tasting room followed quickly by an increase in production.

Infinite Ale Works

Infinite Ale Works is a brewery in planning and soon in production in Ocala. The brewery is connected to Pie on Broadway Pizzeria and looks to be Ocala's first craft brewery.

Mad Beach Craft Brewing Company

Mad Beach Craft Brewing Company has been working to set up shop in the John's Pass and Treasure Island area of Saint Petersburg.

Mad Beach (short for Madeira Beach) has submitted paperwork for a federal brewer's permit, is in the planning stages of brewing and has opened its doors as a craft beer tap room. The brewery is affiliated with the Florida Winery.

Auger Park Brewing Company

Founded by Adam Lenfest and Matthew McKinnon, Auger Park Brewing Company is a community brewpub that has announced intentions of opening in Tampa.

Late Start Brewery

Late Start Brewery developed from an idea that cousins Jordan Copher and Tyler Sankey had about brewing their own beer. When Tyler began purchasing beer equipment and perfecting recipes in his garage, Late Start Brewery was born. While the guys are interested in expanding into a brewery, Florida law currently prohibits their selling beer from their ten-gallon garage brewery. The cousins accept donations for beer they brew and are seeking to perfect their own unique take on beer styles.

Ludwig Brewing

Ludwig Brewing is a brewery in development in Saint Petersburg. Tom Ludwig and Emily Dayan are Saint Petersburgers seeking to open a brewery.

Discount Beer, Near Beer, and Florida's Largest Craft Beer Company

Brewing in Central Florida

CENTRAL FLORIDA'S BREWING PAST

Orlando, and eastern Central Florida, did not become a well-known part of Florida's beer history until late in the twentieth century. Orlando had one brewery that made its mark on the state, then another that tried to resurrect the defunct brewery, but it would not be until 2003 that the seeds of one of Florida's largest breweries would be planted in the small city of Melbourne.

Orlando's brewing history started on the shores of a small lake in pre-Disney Orlando. The Atlantic Brewing Company began op-

Atlantic Ale poster. Courtesy of Michael Zane.

erations as another in a chain of breweries under the Atlantic Brewing Company's banner, which owned several breweries throughout the southern United States: according to an Atlantic Brewing Company matchbook there were breweries in southern cities like Chattanooga, Atlanta, Orlando, Charlotte, and Norfolk. The Atlantic Brewing Company in Orlando made beer, ale, and bock in multiple sizes and multiple formats.

Once Atlantic Brewery succumbed to the undertow, a brave entrepreneur decided to try his hand at the brewery business. New York businessman Joe A. Ringenback purchased the brewery and equipment that Atlantic had abandoned and rechristened the brewery "Marlin Brewing Company."

Marlin Brewing Company only swam in the beer stream for a few short years, and now only cans remain to mark the brewery's existence. "Marlin's White Label Beer" prided itself on being light and dry, Marlin's "Green Hornet Ale" was "the ale with a zip." After the Marlin Brewing Company was fished out in 1956, the Orlando area continued without a local brewery until the late 1980s. Florida brewpub laws were then changed to allow for restaurants to manufacture a maximum of 2,000 barrels of beer for people to drink onsite only. It was then that the first rediscovery of local beer took place, with one exception.

Orlando's Far Point Brewery

In the early 1970s, construction began on the lone brewery that opened between the Great Extinction of the 1960s and the modern era. This brewery managed to fill a niche in Florida beer: discount beer. L. N. Duncan moved to Auburndale, Florida, a small town that grew up around the South Florida Railroad. The city is east of Lakeland, on the way to Orlando off Interstate 4, and would decide Florida's stake in future elections. Duncan had previously worked at the Queen's City Brewery in Maryland and saw an opening in the grip that Milwaukee and Saint Louis had on the Sunshine State: no one was making low-priced, economy beers. Everyone who was making beer was sending it to Orlando and other parts of Florida, but Duncan thought that he could eliminate some freight costs and make generic, store-brand beers for large state retailers like Albertson's and Winn-Dixie. In essence, Duncan wanted to make and sell the cheapest stuff on the shelf.

Construction began at Duncan's brewery in 1972, and it opened the next year. Duncan's confidence in his brewery was so complete that he opened with a three-hundred-barrel brewing system at his brewery and won contracts he sought. For Albertson's, one of the state's top grocery retailers at the time, Duncan made Master's Choice and Master's Choice Light Beer. For ABC Liquors, he manufactured Fischer's Old German Style Beer and Fischer's Light, as well as ABC, ABC Light, ABC Ale, and ABC Malt Liquor. Duncan also made his own brand of beer, which he called "Dunk's."

Duncan began to diversify his operation by brewing a beverage similar to the near-beer brewed during Prohibition. This new beverage was Malta, a cereal, nonalcoholic beverage that was popular in Cuba and Latin America. Duncan made Malta for South American and Cuban markets; then he also produced a beer by the same name for Cuban exiles.

Much stayed the same at Duncan's brewery until the 1980s, when he decided to sell operations in the brewery to the G. Heileman Brewery, which wanted to market its wares in Florida. In May of 1980, Duncan sold his brewery to Heileman, who then changed the name to the Florida Brewery. Duncan's brewery proved to be too small for Heileman, who claimed that efficiency was too difficult to maintain. Duncan then bought his brewery back from the larger company, kept the name, and weathered the tempestuous competition that the major breweries were bringing, but like so many of his forebears, Duncan would be buffeted by other brands of beer.

As the '80s began to close, the major breweries were introducing their "light" beers, whose price tag encroached on Duncan's budget beer niche. Duncan would turn the company over to Max Duncan, who would then sell the brewery to Ramon Campos, who would continue the tradition of brewing Malta. As of the mid 1990s, Campos and his son claimed 250,000 barrels of beer sold annually and seven million dollars in sales in a time when brewpubs and microbreweries were trying to establish themselves.

Campos introduced several new microbrews to the market to generate sales in the South Florida market and he also brewed a private label beer for the Hooters chain, a European style beer called Gator Lager, and Bayside Beer. In February of 2003 the Florida Brewery stopped brewing alcoholic beer in order to focus its efforts on brewing the more profitable Malta from L. N. Duncan's original brewing system.

Rebirth then Renaissance

Orlando waited until the late 1980s for a local brewery. John Stuart, who currently brews at Natty Greene's brewery in North Carolina, began his brewing career at the Winter Park Brewing Company in 1988, around the corner from the current location of Cask and Larder. The Winter Park Brewing Company was taken over by The Mill Restaurant and Brewery in the 1990s. The Mill became a statewide brewery chain, in the same vein as Hops Restaurant, but not as prolific in locations. The Mill would open locations in Jacksonville, Miami, and Tallahassee, spreading the brewpub concept around Florida, Georgia, and Alabama to eighteen stores from 1980 to 2000.

The legacy of The Mill Restaurant lasts into the twenty-first century as a former home brewer began a challenge for other home brewers in the state. John Cheek, who began as the president of Central Florida Home Brewers, helped The Mill Restaurant in Winter Park host the Sunshine Challenge Home Brew Competition. How far has this event progressed? John Cheek is now the president of the Orlando Brewing Company, and the Sunshine Challenge is still hosted annually in Orlando.

In June of 1992, another upstart brewery began operations in Orlando, this time out of the kitchen of a Holiday Inn, and spread to take over the Kirkman Road location of The Mill. Beach Brewing would be one of the craft breweries in the 1990s striving to bring back local beer. The small craft brewery was meant to be a production brewery, one that just sold kegs and beer for distribution. The brewery's vice president was quoted in a newspaper article talking about how he and his employees hit the City Beautiful's pavement networking with bars and restaurants to sell Beach Brewing's liquid sunshine. Those efforts were met with about fifty commitments. Of those fifty commitments, only two businesses actually purchased beer. Beach Brewing would then trust in consumer education, teaching the general populace about the finer points of craft beer, and sales slowly increased. Beach Brewing would ultimately fold around 2000.

The next mile marker on the highway of Orange County's craft beer identity comes by way of the frigid north. Shipyard Brewing

Company of Maine had its eyes on becoming a staple beer in the hands of thirsty Floridians, so they wanted to create a unique pub experience. Shipyard originally tried to purchase the extinct Florida Brewing Company of Ybor City in 1999 but quickly decided that the renovations would cost too much money without delivering the pub experience the brewery was looking for. That pub experience was built into the Orlando Airport, however, and was run by Shipyard brewer Ron Raike. Since the Shipyard Airport Pub was actually making beer in the airport, the brewing system had to be quite small. The airport pub lasted from about 1997 until after the millennium.

In 2003, Florida's largest small brewery set down roots as the Indian River Beverage Company. Indian River Beverage Company began modestly as a contract brewery, but the business-savvy ownership saw opportunity where other breweries were caught in a maelstrom. In 2003, right around the time when Ybor City Brewing Company was closing its doors, YCBC's owner, Humberto Perez, was looking for a way to continue brewing his historic beers while allowing his own brewery to close. Perez then contract brewed Ybor City Brewing Company's beers through the Indian River Beverage Company. As the beverage company began to work through its contracts, many other Florida breweries were beginning to fold and close their doors, but business-savvy Humberto Perez wanted to acquire these brands and brew them again. Perez acquired the rights and recipes to Key West Brewing and Miami Brewing as both breweries were going out of business. Perez then held the recipes and continued brewing his beers at the Florida Beer Company. When Ybor City Brewing Company ran into troubles with distribution issues and subsequently folded, Florida Beer Company purchased all of the brands and recipes from Perez. These brands and contract brewing would help to propel Florida Beer Company into the top spot of Florida breweries, as the brewery utilized many of the brands Perez had purchased in order to make its name. Key

West Sunset Ale, Southernmost Wheat, Hurricane Reef Pale Ale, and Hurricane Reef Raspberry Wheat Ale along with the Ybor City Brewing Company brands helped catapult Florida Beer Company into its current spot as the biggest craft brewery in Florida (if Yuengling is not counted as a craft brewery). Florida Beer Company would help other Florida breweries to get their beers into bottles as they were getting off the ground, contract beers like Holy Mackerel and Orange Blossom Pilsner, which were both initially brewed at Florida Beer Company. Florida Beer Company would also be one of the first craft breweries in chain stores and Publix and would give Florida its first mixed pack of beer.

After the millennium, many of Florida's older breweries passed into memory, but a new class has come in to take up the mantle of those who brewed in Florida's past, before the beer-drinking public had discovered craft beer.

CENTRAL FLORIDA'S BREWING PRESENT

Orlando Brewing Company

Brewery
1301 Atlanta Ave., Orlando 32806
(407) 872-1117
http://orlandobrewing.com
Open 7 days a week; tours Monday through Saturday

Orlando Brewing Company is Orlando's first brewery to open its doors after the wave of Florida craft breweries closing near the millennium. It is located in the industrial park off Atlanta Avenue in Orlando, just before the bustling I-4 corridor winds its way through the City Beautiful. The brewery's tap room creates a haven in the ever-expanding metropolis that is Orlando.

Brewery president John Cheek began Orlando Brewing Company as Orlando Brewing Partners back in April of 2006. Before 2006, John was a prominent member of the home brewing community on Florida's Space Coast, helping to found Orlando's home brew club in 1989. John talks of the time when Orlando in particular and Florida in general were without any decent beer at arm's length (McGuire's and others have been around that long, but no one wanted to drive eight hours for a beer). It took only seventeen years for John to move from making beer at home to opening Orlando's first organic brewery, and he even invented a now-crucial piece of home brewing equipment along the way (the carbonator cap). When it opened, Orlando Brewing was brewing about 1,000 barrels of beer during its first year. John and his brewery staff also shouldered the immense burden of educating Florida consumers on the quality of craft beer. After all, Orlando had been without a distributing craft brewery for decades. Orlando Brewing has been increasing production ever since opening, producing 1,724 barrels of beer in 2012 and 1,800 barrels in 2013. The brewery is now brewing about seventeen batches each month to satisfy the eighteen taps in the brewery, in addition to accounts in the six counties that Orlando Brewing currently satisfies.

Orlando Brewing's core brands are all bottled and available on draft at its tasting room. Orlando Brewing offers blond ale, red ale, pale ale, brown ale, dry black porter, European Pilsner, and Aniscoria Single Malt Ale at the brewery. The brewery has a seasonal set of beers (dubbed the Brewers Selection) and two new series rotating ales: an IPA series and a Violator series. The Brewers Selection series rotates seasonal beers while following the Bavarian Purity Law. The Violator series—violent as it sounds—merely refers to beers that violate the Bavarian Purity Law, such as pumpkin ale or chocolate stout. Finally, the IPA series guarantees that hop fans who visit Orlando Brewing will never leave thirsty.

Orlando Brewing is Florida's first organic brewery, and they are proud that their beers are well made and brewed according to their style. As their distribution has currently hit a sweet spot, Orlando Brewing's beers are on draft only at accounts across Florida, but much of the experimental and seasonal beer is freshest and best at the source.

Mount Dora/Rocking Rabbit Brewery

Brewpub
405 South Highland St., Mount Dora 32757
(352) 406-2924
http://mountdorabrewing.com
Open 7 days a week

Mount Dora Brewing is one of two breweries in Lake County, and it shares space with a cozy restaurant that also has live music. The small brewery keeps a few beers on draft, enough to satisfy pub and brewery patrons in this lively and off-the-beaten-path Florida city.

Mount Dora Brewing offers lunch fare along with its ales from the only spot in Florida that can be considered a "mountain." Filled with antique stores, walking space, and small eclectic shops, Mount Dora has something for everyone in the family.

Mount Dora Brewing offers its standard lineup with some black-and-tan-esque blends after the fancy of their local customers. The standard-bearers for the brewery are the Beauclair Blonde Ale, a filtered and malty blonde ale and lightest of Mount Dora's beers at 7 percent alcohol; the Rocking Rabbit Red Ale, an Irish-style red ale that's sweet and malty, using some local honey in the beer, with notes of herbal bitterness finishing at 8 percent alcohol; and finally the Pistolville Porter, an unfiltered porter with chocolate and caramel malt and dark brown sugar for a deep and sweet wallop at 9.9 percent alcohol. The beers may be on the higher side of gravity, but the pub has plenty of fresh sandwiches and wraps (and dinner on the weekends) if the beers get to be a bit strong.

Mount Dora Brewing is slightly off the regular Florida ale trail, but is a destination brewery that serves a few homemade beers with its food. It will not be too long before Mount Dora could be looking at a beery triangle like Dunedin, Saint Petersburg, and Jacksonville. Until that point, Mount Dora and the Rocking Rabbit are happy to go steady together.

Big River Grille and Brewing Works

Brewpub
2101 North Epcot Resort Blvd., Lake Buena Vista 32830
(407) 560-0253
http://bigrivergrille.com
Open 7 days a week

Located just behind Disney's Hollywood Studios, nestled into Disney's Boardwalk is this low-key brewpub owned by CraftWorks, which owns the Gordon Biersch brewpub–chain that produces ales in its restaurants. Like other Gordon Biersch pubs, A1A Ale Works and Seven Bridges Grille and Brewery among them, Big River Grille keeps the standard GB beers on but also allows the brewer to improvise on his own draft line. And also like other GB brewpubs, Big River's head brewer is a diamond in the rough who prides himself on his creative beers.

Big River's brewer, Kent Waugh, brews the beer to keep the tourists and Disney visitors happy, but he also does wonders with the one tap line left to him. When visiting Big River Grille, keep an eye out for something out of the ordinary from Kent: anything from a

chocolate stout to a whiskey barrel–aged brown ale to an espresso stout. These beers are often offered in a limited run, and when they are gone there is no more for the foreseeable future.

Big River will always have the normal spectrum of beers on draft: a red ale, a pale ale, a brown ale, a stout, and a lager. These beers keep the seasonal friends from getting thirsty. When the witching hour arrives and a new beer goes on, look for a fresh, well-made beer crafted a few feet away from the bar in the glass-enclosed brewery that exists within the confines of the restaurant.

Big River brings a craft brewery into Mickey Mouse's backyard. Getting to the pub is a simple matter of either hopping on a boat to Disney's Boardwalk or going for a spirited walk. If the pub food was not enough, then Big River's taps should be just the thing to help tourists and locals alike find a second wind for going back into the Disney theme parks.

Florida Beer Company

Brewery
200 Imperial Blvd., Cape Canaveral 32920
(321) 728-4114
http://floridabeer.com
Open 7 days a week

The Florida Beer Company has been running continuously since 2003, in its first incarnation as Indian River Beverage Company. Once the brewery changed its name, it moved into the previous facility in Melbourne and in 2013 moved into its new home, a 60,000-square-foot brewery and adjoining tasting room.

The Florida Beer Company began as one of Florida's first production and contract breweries since the brewery mass extinction of the 1960s. When the Indian River Beverage Company began in 1997, its main focus was on brewing other people's beers on its system. Jack Owen has been Florida Beer Company's brewer since the

company's inception and was a member of the first graduating class of the University of California at Berkeley's Brewing Science Program. Owen's steady and traditional approach to beer has helped fuel the brewery's growth. Once the brewery solidified its place in Florida's beer pantheon, it slowly increased pace and growth to become the largest craft brewery in Florida, behind Yuengling (and there is an argument over whether a small brewery can be one that brews several million barrels each year). Florida Beer Company has helped many other breweries brew their beer without having to buy equipment and in the process has grown into the need for a new facility.

Since Florida Brewing Company owns the recipes for some of Florida's most historic ales and lagers, the first trip can seem a bit confusing. On any day of the week, Florida Brewing Company might be pouring La Tropical Lager (the same one that traces its history back through Cuba, although in a roundabout way), or Kelly's Cider from the first cidery in Florida, Gaspar's Porter (an old Ybor City Brewing Company recipe), or Hurricane Reef Lager from the defunct Miami Brewing Company. These beers all reside within the Florida Beer Company portfolio and are distributed throughout Florida, South Carolina, Virginia, Saint Thomas, and New York. On draft and in bottles are the standard beers of Florida Beer Company: Swamp Ape IPA, a hop-forward 10 percent beast of an IPA; Southernmost Wheat, a 5 percent Belgian-style white ale liquid homage to the Conch Republic of Key West brewed with key lime; the light, bready, and easy-drinking 5.1 percent ABV Florida Lager; and the amber colored, 4.8 percent ABV, and lightly hopped Key West Sunset Ale.

Thanks to FBC's expansion, the brewery redesigned labels, re-released some historical beers, and in 2014 opened to the public a brand new, state-of-the-art 60,000-square-foot facility with plans for making barrel-aged and even sour beers. The Florida Beer Company moved down the street to Cape Canaveral, and the brewery had the uncanny distinction of being one of Florida's oldest breweries in Florida's newest facility.

The Hourglass Brewery

Brewery
255 South Ronald Reagan Blvd., Longwood 32750
(407) 262-0056
http://thehourglassbrewery.com
Open 7 days a week

The Hourglass Brewery lies on a busy stretch of highway in the hamlet of Longwood, north of Orlando. The small brewery runs a tasting room in the front, with a small beer garden off the back of the nondescript house it occupies. This brewery, so named because it keeps running out of time, is soon to run out of space as it keeps growing larger and more popular with the locals.

The Hourglass Brewery is Seminole County's only craft brewery. Part of the growing number of Florida breweries opened in 2012, Hourglass Brewery started its beer on a hundred-gallon brewing

system that yields about three barrels of beer at any given time. Head brewer Sky Conley and his brewing partner Brett Mason man the brewery and aim to turn out small artisanal batches of beer as fast as the community will drink them out of the brewery's taps.

Along with pale ales and IPAs, look for the taps to flow with beers like a Table Milk Beer, a style-bending beer that blends milk sugar with a simple table beer, like a session ale. Look also for Belgian-style sours and smoked beers with raisins in the mix, too. Sweet, sour, and savory flavors all flow from the same taps, and the tiny tap room gets hopped up on weekends when the food trucks swing by to serve dinner.

While Longwood is not known as a beer mecca, a great pint can turn a local into a craft beer enthusiast, and any local brewery has the potential to become a favorite haunt. Look for more news to come from Hourglass as they expand to a ten barrel system and add hundreds of bottle release to their offerings.

Cask and Larder

Brewpub
565 West Fairbanks Ave., Winter Park 32789
(321) 280-4200
http://caskandlarder.com
Open 7 days a week

Cask and Larder is craft beer on a date with a five-star restaurant, looking to get married. Owners James and Julie Petrakis thought up the concept of Cask and Larder—a southern kitchen with craft beer brought to its fullest potential by a brewer with decades of experience. To that end, they sought the expertise of twenty-year brewer Ron Raike, a stalwart brewer in the Florida craft beer environs. Located in the Winter Park area of Orlando, Cask and Larder seeks to provide a food and beer experience unlike any other.

While the food at Cask and Larder is the purview of the chefs, the beer is solely the reality of Ron Raike, and Ron has stepped up his game to the level of the food at Cask and Larder. Ron's attention to the minutiae of brewing begins outside the brewhouse at the water filter. Ron has studied water chemistry, and because water is the main ingredient in beer, when a beer is made to mimic a historical style, like a Belgian witbier, then Ron pays attention to the unique qualities present in the water of the city where the beer originated. Ron will then harden or soften the water to the specifications of the historical city via a reverse osmosis water filter, and proceed with brewing. With a five-barrel brewing system, Ron is able to stock up enough beers to satisfy the restaurant customers while also being able to rotate the taps for Cask and Larder's regulars. In fact, Ron tries to create a different experience at the taps during every visit to

the restaurant. Some of the styles may be the same, but the ingredients will not be. For instance, Cask and Larder may always have an IPA on draft, but that IPA may differ in hops or a Belgian witbier may have fruits added to the beer that change with every visit. Just as a chef's menu will change, so too will the brewer's menu, and at Cask and Larder the two may change in unison and complement each other.

While Cask and Larder offer keg sales and limited distribution, currently the best variety of C & L beer is available through the taps at the copper pipe in Cask and Larder's bar. The beer menu's workhorse is a Belgian wit dubbed Southern Wit. That witbier will change in recipe from time to time and possibly incorporate different spices, grains, or fruits, but will be the constantly working core beer. After the wit, Ron will keep an IPA on draft as well as a beer that is fuller in body and alcohol. The bar has a total of eight taps, so variety is to be anticipated. Outside of the restaurant, Cask and Larder's Southern Wit along with Red Drum Amber Ale, Five Points IPA, and Broken Ladder Pale Ale all see limited distribution in a small circle of Orlando.

Just like the food environment that Cask and Larder is trying to create, the restaurant and its brewer are showing diners that each beer can have a story; each beer can be crafted just for the meal on the table.

Bugnutty Brewing Company

Brewery
715 North Courtenay Parkway, Merritt Island 32953
(321) 452-4460
http://www.bugnutty.com
Closed Monday and Tuesday

What do rocket scientists do in their spare time? They brew great beer. Bugnutty Brewing Company is another of the Space Coast's craft breweries, the second founded by a former NASA employee. A trio of friends, Michael, Shawn, and Jon began Bugnutty Brewing Company; Michael works at NASA and Shawn retired from the air force, where he also worked on jets and rockets. The brewery opened on Friday, September 13, 2013, and has quickly been gaining traction in Merritt Island and beyond.

While one meaning of "bugnutty" is "to have feelings of frustration," in the case of the brewery, it is "a state of overwhelming delight and rapturous emotion." Bugnutty brews its beers on a small two-barrel brewing system and has several house beers on draft at any given time.

Bugnutty's current lineup of beers starts with Red, Wheat, and Blue, a Glacier-hopped amber-hued wheat ale with blueberries added to pair with light citrus. Next is Sticky Foot, an American pale ale with Simcoe hops added for notes of apricot and stone fruit with some light tropical fruit. An American IPA, Zeus Will Smite Thee has rye malt for some spicy rye notes along with a backbone and Galena, Zythos, and Ahtanum hops for hoppiness. Suzi's Red Belly Ale is a malty red ale that dials in hop bitterness as well. Mike's Milk Stout rounds out the flavor spectrum with a bit of sweetness added to flavors of chocolate and coffee. The lineup of taps is ever expanding and now includes a blonde ale, an American strong ale, a porter, and a pilsner.

Bugnutty began limited distribution of Zeus Will Smite Thee and Red, Wheat, and Blue in waves around Brevard County.

Intracoastal Brewing Company

Brewery
652 West Eau Gallie Boulevard, Melbourne 32935
(321) 872-7395
http://www.intracoastalbrewingcompany.com
Closed Tuesday

Intracoastal Brewing Company takes its name from a Space Coast icon: the Intracoastal Waterway. The brewery's logo is the red and green of the channel markers that guide sailors through the waterway just like beer guides patrons through the brewery. Intracoastal Brewing Company graces the Eau Gallie Arts District as a new hangout for locals. Like many other breweries, it is licensed as a tasting room and is not permitted to serve food, so folks are encouraged to bring along their own food or enjoy the local food trucks that may pay a visit.

Intracoastal Brewing Company is another jewel in the brewing crown of Brevard County. The brewery's owners wanted to take the feel of a craft brewery, usually located in an industrial part of town, and maneuver it into a more publicly visible area. The resulting brewery has its home in a 3,000-square-foot brick building with several picnic tables for spreading out, a few television sets for sports fans, and dedicated conversation areas.

At any given time, Intracoastal will have up to eight house-brewed beers on draft. Intracoastal beers range from a pale ale and lemonade blended shandy called Shandelicious to a red session IPA called Red Hoppy'd Stepchild to a citrus-forward IPA called Dragon Point IPA to a porter dubbed Port Canaveral; Intracoastal has barley ships for every craft beer sailor.

Cocoa Beach Brewing Company

Brewery
150 North Atlantic Ave., Cocoa Beach 32931
(321) 613-2941
http://cocoabeachbrewingcompany.com
Open 7 days a week

Cocoa Beach Brewing Company has made a nest for itself just a few short blocks from the rolling Atlantic waves in the tourist spot of Cocoa Beach. The tiny brewery and adjacent tasting room look to the unsuspecting eye like another beachfront bungalow, but the brewery seeks to please both locals and tourists alike with local beer on tap and in bottles.

Cocoa Beach Brewing Company was born in 2009 from the sweat and ingenuity of a rocket scientist and his wife. Chris and Tracy McCall took up the brewing mantle and chose to put their brewery and tasting room in one of the oldest houses in Cocoa Beach. In its previous life, the building was military housing for the Banana River Naval Air Station. When Chris and Tracy came into the place, they renovated the housing portion for the brewery's tasting room and the garage for the brewery. The brewery has since expanded, adding on to the garage, and Cocoa Beach Brewing Company can now brew four-barrel batches of beer, a jump from their original fifty-five gallon capabilities.

Cocoa Beach Brewing Company is available on draft and in twenty-two-ounce bottles throughout Central Florida, Gainesville, and Jacksonville. Their core beers in twenty-two-ounce bottles are the malty and citrusy 6.6 percent alcohol Cocoa Beach Pale Ale, the roasty and dark chocolate flavors of Not Just Some Oatmeal Stout, and the citrusy and piney 888 IPA, so named for its 8 percent alcohol presence. Cocoa Beach Brewing also keeps a few taps in the tasting room for "R & D Beers": limited batches and small runs. Some of the beers that rotate through on draft this way are the Key Lime Cerveza, a lighter color beer brewed with Pilsner malt, and the malty and earthy Von Braun Ale, named for Werner Von Braun, the German rocket scientist who was a pioneer in the field and led America to expand its space program.

Cocoa Beach Brewing Company is one of those cozy Florida bars housed in a converted beach house minutes from the waves and sand. They pour the brewery's standards and one-offs that will never see distribution. They take beach beer to a new level and allow parched tourists the chance to try a craft beer while on vacation from everywhere else.

Charlie and Jake's Brewery Grille

Brewpub
6300 North Wickham Rd., Melbourne 32940
(321) 752-7675
http://cjbrewery.com
Open 7 days a week

Charlie and Jake's, a storefront brewpub in Melbourne, Florida, is a brewery attached to a strip mall in the Suntree area. The interior offers a comfortable earth-toned lounge that provides a clear view to the brewery area. Charlie and Jake's offers southern-style barbeque with local beer brewed on site and many folks only too happy to discuss any aspect of the pub.

Since opening in 1996, Charlie and Jake's began brewing the following year and has been anchoring craft beer in the Harbor City of Melbourne ever since. The brewery stands in a glass-enclosed area of the restaurant and pub, and brewer Todd Furbeck works zymurgical magic. The brewery pumps the beer into serving tanks and then the beer goes right into the taps. The place itself has been renovated since opening, and now it seems like an airy café from a Hemingway story. The laid-back establishment has televisions sprinkled throughout, but many points in the place are enjoyable free from TV.

Charlie and Jake's is more than meets the eye. Their core beers are very approachable, even if Charlie and Jake's is one's first craft beer experience. The Wickham Wheat is citrusy with notes of bread and some earthy hops. The sweet lager, Harbor City Gold, gives a crisp accompaniment to many of the savory foods at Charlie and Jake's. The hoppy amber ale called Indian River Red gives a nice amount of caramel and some complementary citrus hops. Finally, the nutty Brown Bottom Brown Ale bares its teeth with a hint of earthy hops. While the core beers are dependable, Todd continues to play with his brewing system and pours out both seasonal and limited beers. A trip to Charlie and Jake's may yield a pint of anything from a light and fruity hefeweizen to a witbier with cranberries to a vanilla bean porter and most styles in between. A trip at the right time of the year could provide a sip of the Anniversary Ale dry hopped three times with Cascade hops—the same ale that won a silver medal at the 1997 Great American Beer Festival.

Charlie and Jake's is a local watering hole that has expanded to include some nice beers to pair with BBQ. This local haunt is always worth a stop because the brewery does tap experimental beers periodically like a Green Apple Saison and the Best Florida Beer Gold Medal Double Trouble Barleywine. Charlie and Jake's has more than sauces brewing in their homey pub.

New Smyrna Beach Brewing Company

Brewery
112 Sams Avenue, New Smyrna Beach 32168
(386) 957-3802
http://www.newsmyrnabrewing.com
Closed Monday through Wednesday

New Smyrna Beach Brewing Company is one of the few craft beer strongholds between Orlando and Jacksonville.

New Smyrna Beach Brewing Company is the project of two-year home brewer Chris Coyle and his fiancée, Sara Lammers.

The brewery is a three-barrel brewing system. The first beer Coyle put on draft was Inlet, his amber ale. Other brews include Coronado cream ale, Shark Bite pale ale, and Shark Attack IPA. Coyle wants his rotating beers to mirror Florida's weather patterns: beers lighter in intensity in the summer and darker and spicier brews in the winter. Several guest taps are filled with additional Florida craft beers.

BREWERIES IN FERMENTATION

Orchid Island Brewing Company

Orchid Island Brewing is located in Vero Beach on the Space Coast of Florida. The brewery brews with local Indian River citrus and highlights the citrus character in many of its beers. Orchid Island brews on a three-barrel system and plans to open in 2015.

Redlight Redlight Beer Parlour

The venerable Orlando craft beer bar has been serving craft beer in the City Beautiful for years now, and owner Brent Hernandez has put out the word that he is ready to take the next step. Known for his tart Berliner weisses and eye-puckering sour beers, Hernandez has shared his home brew with patrons of the bar; now he is ready to take ownership of a small brewing system and supply the bar, and possibly Orlando, with his beers.

Mermaid Juice

Mermaid Juice, the combination antique store and craft beer bar has dreamed about a brewery for many years. Mermaid Juice owner Daneux Narrow has been trying to put together a brewing system for the beer bar for a while. Narrow has decided to put the pilot system for the brewery in neighboring DeLand in order to allow the brewery space to grow.

Local Brews after Jax Beer

Brewing in Florida's Northeast

NORTHEAST FLORIDA'S BREWING PAST

The city of Jacksonville's brewing history starts with several businessmen whose names have been lost to the annals of history. Journals and letters of the day report that the newborn town of Jacksonville served beer in saloons dating back to about 1878. The brewery that all Jacksonville natives seem to have a clear recollection of is the Jax Brewery. The Jax Brewery was begun by a German immigrant named William Ostner, who, according to his son, had originally wanted to be an innkeeper. After apprenticing at an inn in Mannheim, Ostner saw how illustrious the life of the local beer brewer was, and decided that a change of professions was in order. Ostner set off for brewing school in Berlin, and after he graduated in 1904, he set sail for New York. Initially working as a chemist in New York, Ostner struck out for work in Saint Louis, Missouri, gaining employment at the Union Brewery, eventually becoming the brewmaster. In 1911, Ostner married the daughter of the

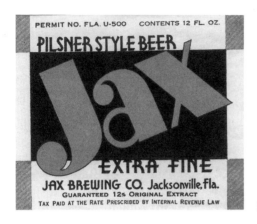

PERMIT NO. FLA. U-500   CONTENTS 12 FL. OZ.

PILSNER STYLE BEER

Jax

EXTRA FINE

JAX BREWING CO. Jacksonville, Fla.
GUARANTEED 12% ORIGINAL EXTRACT
TAX PAID AT THE RATE PRESCRIBED BY INTERNAL REVENUE LAW

Jax Beer poster. Courtesy of Michael Zane.

prominent Schorr brewing family, who suggested that Jacksonville, Florida, would be an ideal spot to open a brewery, especially since the city had just voted against statewide prohibition the previous year. Ostner decided to take his skills and education, a few industrious investors, his personal friend and fellow German immigrant Jacob Bongner, and several prominent citizens of Duval County to Jacksonville and on June 9, 1913, saw the groundbreaking for the Jacksonville Brewing Company, 16th Street west of Myrtle Avenue.

Jacksonville's brewery began modestly with Bongner as president and Ostner as brewer. According to minutes from the shareholders meeting a month after the groundbreaking, the brewery was slated to cost $182,000 to build, and $101,000 worth of stock had been subscribed. The capacity of the plant would be 30,000 barrels annually brewed on a 150-barrel brewing system provided by the Goetz Company of Chicago. After matters were settled, the first beers of the Jacksonville Brewing Company were sent to market. The first and most infamous beer was a lager dubbed "Jax Beer." The other two beers available via the H. W. Metcalf Company (distributor) were Royal Palm Beer and Old Fashioned Wurzburger. A keg of Jax cost $8.00 and 10 dozen bottles cost an even $7.00. Royal Palm cost $10 for 10 dozen bottles (Old Wurzburger would have been similar in cost to Royal Palm). These beers would all have been made with a lager yeast according to the German tradition, and according to the custom of the day, the beers were tested by a chemist and certified as "pure." This affirmation appears on most pre-Prohibition Florida beers, causing natural curiosity about any beers that were ever rejected by these tests.

The whole of Jacksonville then saw economic depression from 1914 to 1916, and Jacksonville's brewery was no exception. To help operations, both Bongner and Ostner agreed to cut their salaries by half until the brewery recovered. After 1915, the brewery would reach profits over $3,000 per month, and in 1916 that number rose to about $5,000 per month. By 1917, the brewery had retired its debts, purchased new labeling equipment, and even bought Bongner a new car. At this point, the brewery was paying its employees based on union wages. By this contract, each week the brewery paid $21 to brewers, $15 to bottlers, $16 to coopers, $19 to drivers, with a chief engineer making $18 every seven days. The brewery was on its way to recovery, especially after a military camp was established in Jacksonville and up to 27,000 men were stationed after war was declared on Germany.

The same soldiers that would seem to be a balm to the ailing brewery would also become their bane. It was reported that Jacksonville developed a significant problem with drunken sailors listlessly wandering the city on any given Saturday, so the base commander took action. He asked that Jacksonville become a dry city or he would place it off-limits to the troops. At the risk of losing military business, the city voted to become dry on May 14, 1918. The brewery and its owners read the writing on the wall, and the investors instructed the president to cut their losses and find a buyer. In July of 1918, the brewery was offered to the Piel Brothers Brewery in New York for a minimum of $180,000.

On July 25, 1918, the operation changed its name to The Jacksonville Ice and Cold Storage Company to reflect a more diversified operation. The brewery always had an ice plant and cold storage, but now the brewery invested in improvements to the ice business as its haven. After all, both operations could dwell on the existing well and facilities. The brewery was seeking a long-term solution to the downturn in the economy; with the clarity of hindsight, this type of investment would help the brewery weather a much larger storm on the horizon.

With beer no longer bringing in the groceries, the brewery-turned-ice-plant sought to remain in business, the best business Ostner and Bongner could find. Toward this end the plant then retired $30,000 worth of outstanding debts and restored the salaries of the president and brewer. In 1919 the investors voted to construct an ice cream plant, which was completed that same year, and the idea of making grapefruit and orange juice was also brought up. By the onset of National Prohibition in 1920, $75,000 had been spent on new investments with only $21,000 of that capital recorded as debt. Part of the new business venture also included the addition of contracts for ginger ale and root beer. By 1921 business was going so well that the ice plant doubled and investments seemed to be bringing in a good return.

In March of 1924, Jacob Bongner passed away and William Ostner took over as president of operations at the one-time brewery. Ostner worked to add two new cold storage plants in three years, expansions costing over $100,000. The corporation rewarded his efforts with a $6,000 annual raise, and they also insured his life for $25,000. The next year an article appeared in the *Jacksonville Journal* about the company. In that article it is worth noting that the former brewery was making three near beers: Florida Export, Jax, and Old Fashioned Dark. Each of these beers had a counterpart in the brewery's former production, now made to contain only trace amounts of alcohol, as was legal at the time. The ice plant had a daily capacity of 120 tons, soon to be increased to 180 tons. The plant produced all of this on a tract of land 330 feet by 140 feet, employing forty-five people on a monthly payroll of $45,000. Breweries across the country were shutting their doors and selling anything they could to remain afloat, but not in Jacksonville.

Diversifying operations before and during Prohibition proved lucrative for the former brewery, although Jax would make one more Prohibition mainstay that would gain them far more attention: near beer. While many breweries across the country made near beer to help them through Prohibition, Jacksonville Ice and Cold Storage made near beer by first making full-strength beer, then pumping the product back into the kettle and boiling off the alcohol. In an interview with beer historian Kip Sharpe, William Ostner's son William A. Ostner disclosed the process and the attention it brought the company, since at one point in the process there would be full-strength beer on the premises. The younger Ostner said:

> Prominent people such as police chiefs, fire chiefs, the mayor, newspaper editors, and bankers often came by for real beer. In fact, they came by so often that my father was not getting any work done so he set up Friday afternoons as a time to meet.

Ostner also said that the brewery's sales of near beer turned out better than most, since customers would often take it to a speakeasy and spike it. Apparently the only official businesses that were making money during Prohibition were ice and cold storage. The rest of the business was not the kind that could be put on the books and taxed, but all of the people who would deal with enforcement seemed to forget about such trifles after Friday afternoons. While many were engaged in illicit activities during Prohibition, it is almost admirable that Jax brewery mostly followed the law during these times.

Jacksonville, like many other Florida towns, had its share of rumrunners and speakeasies (including ties to and visits from notorious gangster Al Capone), but the brewery did not sell to speakeasies—it tried to get by on near beer and a diverse operation. Word just got out about its process, and city officials required themselves to do quality assurance testing, only they did it away from prying eyes during preestablished hours at the brewery.

Business looked so good that despite Prohibition and its effects, Ostner's company gained competition. On April 20, 1926, three men incorporated the Jacksonville Brewing Agency. Their mission would be "to manufacture, bottle, and sell pure water, carbonated, both mineral and distilled water, ginger ale, sarsaparilla, and other non-alcoholic beverages . . . dairy products, cold storage . . ." according to the city directory. Like several other would-be breweries, the venture never prospered. Such local competition was not new to anyone in Florida, but in Jacksonville, the former Jacksonville Brewing Company had already dug in its heels and diversified its operations enough to weather Prohibition. Not every brewing-based business was as fortunate or as forward-sighted.

In May of 1933, 3.2 percent alcohol by volume beer became legal in Florida once again, a month behind the rest of America. The Jacksonville Ice and Cold Storage Company had anticipated this move and ordered nine beer tanks in early 1933. In April of the same year, Ostner was authorized to purchase all needed equipment to return to the production of beer. Ads were placed around Jacksonville, and the brewery was made ready to fulfill its frothy destiny again. Ironically, the next meeting of the same board instructed Ostner to negotiate with buyers to sell the plant. After receiving an offer for a million dollars, the board turned down the offer. They felt a one-million-dollar offer was insufficient compared to the potential profits. At the same meeting in July of 1933, the board went further and authorized a bonus for Ostner of fifteen cents per barrel for each barrel sold in excess of 15,000. It would take the brewery less than two years to pay off all debts.

Jax became a local sensation, and the brewery had to brew in double shifts five days a week to keep up with the demand. Business was so good that during the 1930s the brewmaster, John Huskamp, was able to test the waters with new recipes and new possible brands. During this time Jax Brewery produced Ostner's Ale, beer, and stout, Jax Export, Florida Export, Mecca ("the ultimate destination"), Royal Palm, and a beer called Fine's Sparkling Ale on contract for a Georgia beverage supplier.

As the 1930s came to a close, increased production and profitability came to the hard-working Jacksonville brewery. The brewery was able to hire William Gould away from the Wagner and Gould Brewing Companies in Miami and offer him a salary of $400 each month, plus commission. The brewery was currently selling 35,000 barrels each year, and promised Mr. Gould twenty-six cents for each barrel sold over 45,000. Once World War II began, and military presence increased significantly, every brewery in the Sunshine State saw a significant increase in demand, and Jax was no exception. The brewery increased production from 35,000 barrels to 65,000 barrels in 1942, then again in 1943 to 103,000 barrels. It was brewing twice a day, five days a week, and paying its employees in lieu of letting them take vacation. Ninety percent of Jax's beer was put into bottles; the brewery saved money and helped war rations by making its own bottle caps during the war years. In 1942, the brewery reported paying $500,000 in state and federal taxes, $200,000 in payroll, and maintenance on a fleet of trucks that traveled over one million miles.

The New Orleans Connection

In 1935, the brewery hired a legal counsel to sue the Jackson Brewery of New Orleans over the trademark of the name "Jax." The Jackson Brewing Company had named their beer for Jackson Square in the Big Easy and had national ambitions. Jax brewery had named the beer for the town and had regional ambitions. The two reached a compromise: Jax Brewery would have the rights to the name in

Florida and Georgia, and Jackson would have rights to the name everywhere else.

Around the same time the brewery was settling its trademark suit with Jackson Brewing, another New Orleans brewery was coming into hard times—the Old Union Brewery. In 1939, Old Union was forced to close its doors due, they claimed, to the lack of metal to make bottle caps. The New Orleans Brewing Company bought the name and trademarked Old Union's slogan, "Shoot the Works." Around 1941, production of Old Union's beers was contracted out, via an enterprising Jacksonville family, to the Jax Brewery. By 1942, the Jax Brewery was seeing tremendous increases in consumption from month to month, with much of it attributed to the manufacture of Old Union.

In Jacksonville, the years of World War II were good for business. Jax began the 1940s losing about $10,000 selling 32,000 barrels in 1940, but in the span of one year, the brewery was selling 42,000 barrels at a $16,000 profit. The next year, 1943, the brewery would record a $73,000 profit, and that meant a flat $6,000 bonus for William Ostner. The brewery returned some of the money to the community, most notably by building a swimming pool for the local boy scouts, another pool for the girl scouts, and a mess hall for the "colored" scout camp. The end of the war continued to help the brewery, as rationing and materials quotas ended and Ostner's sons returned from war to work at the brewery. Veterans were given hiring preference, and since Jacksonville had a growing population of them, the brewery thrived. In 1948 brewmaster John Huskamp retired from brewing and was awarded a $250 stipend each month for his thirty-four-year service to the brewery. Huskamp would serve as treasurer to the brewery's board of directors until his death in 1959.

Like every other historical brewery in the land of eternal summer, each story has a point where better days were behind them, and a tumble can be seen. For Jax, 1948 was the year when sales started to decline, in this case by up to 25 percent. Sales increased but profits decreased, due in part to rising materials costs, but the ice and cold storage business continued to do well and helped fill the brewery's profit void. In 1951 the brewery decided not to go quietly into the night—it invested in a new label and an advertising campaign in its service area. For most of 1951 the brewery operated at a loss, up to almost $42,000. In 1952 the ad agency was fired. The brewery tried to transition from bottles to cans in 1950, but slowly. It tried to use cone-top cans (cans with the materials of cans, but capped with a crown or bottle cap) at first. The public did not respond well, so in 1953 the brewery added a canning line to accommodate the trend of flat-top cans coming into vogue around this time. Jax beer, Jax ale, Sans Souci (French for "without care"), Old Union, and Rhein King were all put into flat-top cans. The brewery's businessmen began to focus more on the cold storage business in 1953, obtaining contracts from Gerber and Borden dairy to fund a $63,000 expansion.

Competition in Florida became an increasing challenge for Jax, as other regional breweries were also trying new strategies either to gain market share or to prevent their own declines. The Jax Brewery decided to lower the price of its beer below the cost of the national brands (to 20 cents per bottle; it was 5 cents cheaper than the competition). This decrease was detrimental to the brewery's reputation, and locals began to regard Jax as "the cheap stuff." A bandage was put on the cash hemorrhage with the acquisition of a branch in Orlando due in part to the demise of Atlantic Brewing Company.

One story about Jax during this time period warrants revisiting. During the 1950s, bottles were sold individually, and the breweries did all they could to encourage people to buy multiple bottles at one time. Ostner actually went on to purchase 100,000 "durable sacks" from a local hardware store and put the brewery's logo on them. Those sacks would comfortably fit six bottles; other breweries caught on very quickly, and the modern six-pack was born.

The brewery's business continued to decline, and in 1956 the board decided to seek a buyer for the brewery, but few businesses or investors were interested. The best offers that Jax could get were for use of its trademarked names, and the Jackson Brewery of New Orleans bought them (and still holds the name and sells merchandise at the brewery facility). Sale of the names earned the brewery $36,000, and equipment was sold to salvage for $60,000. From 1952 until final dissolution in 1957, the Jax business had lost close to $450,000. The cold storage business continued, and in 1971 the business changed its name to one closely resembling the name during Prohibition, The Jax Cold Storage Company. That business was sold in 1986, and according to the purchaser, Mr. Ostner left everything; it was as if he had just stepped out. The corporation dissolved in 1998, and the buildings were donated. The plant buildings still remain, and as of 2012 they were being used as an electronics recycling plant.

Change came slowly to Jacksonville, but current-day Jacksonville is much different from the Jacksonville of old. Anheuser-Busch opened a brewery in Jacksonville in 1969. It is still open and is one of the only Anheuser-Busch InBev plants to offer public tours. In addition to the national brewery in town, the northeast Florida town boasts a thriving microbrewing community.

Intuition Ale Works

Brewery
720 King Street, Jacksonville 32204
(904) 683-7720
http://intuitionaleworks.com
Closed Sunday and Monday

Intuition Ale Works is a warehouse brewery near the downtown area of Jacksonville. The brewery is situated in part of a neighborhood and part of an industrial area. The brewery also operates two tasting rooms: one adjacent to the brewery and one in a small space off the brewery.

Head brewer and owner, Ben Davis, a convert from the wine industry, began home brewing in college, moved back to Jacksonville with his family in 2008, and founded Intuition. Since Intuition's first brew in 2008, the brewery has expanded distribution in its

draft offerings to Jacksonville, St. John's County and Saint Augustine, and Fernandina Beach and more recently into Tampa Bay.

The brewery also expanded to allow Florida beer lovers to drink Intuition beer at home by adding a canning line to its bag of tricks. Intuition is currently canning its three mainstay beers, I-10 IPA, John Boat Session-Style Kolsch, and People's Pale Ale, on a line that cans approximately seventy cases per hour.

While the production brewery is canning the brewery's flagship beers, the tasting room adjacent to the brewery offers twenty beers from Intuition at any given time. The fifty-four-seat tasting room pours everything from the everyday Intuition beers to more limited offerings like Truck Stop Breakfast, an imperial stout with smoked malt and maple syrup, or The Underdark, an imperial stout aged in Woodford Reserve Bourbon Barrels for eight months. Combine these beers with occasional food trucks at the brewery, and Intuition is quite a beer destination, especially on Underdark Day, a bottle release for the Underdark, a tradition that began in 2014.

Insider Tip: Intuition Ale Works hosts One-off Wednesdays. Every week offers a new and different Intuition beer that may never be seen again.

Bold City Brewing Company

Brewery
2670-7 Rosselle Street, Jacksonville 32204
(904) 379-6551
http://boldcitybrewery.com
Open Thursday, Friday, and Saturday

Bold City Brewing Company is situated at the end of a plaza in an industrial complex near downtown Jacksonville. There is a home brewing store in the same plaza, actually the same one where Bold City's owner bought his home brewing supplies.

The brewery is owned and operated by Brian Miller and Susan Miller, a mother and son pair. Brian is director of brewery operations, and his mother is his business partner in the company, and Bold City is a true family-run business. The Miller family and their close friends are the heart of the business. Brian proudly states that every person on staff is family, or might as well be (as he has "known them forever"). Brian had the idea for the brewery but had to sell his mother on investing in the brewery after she retired from thirty-five years in the insurance industry. Brian achieved this goal by taking his mother to the annual Craft Brewer's Conference. Upon doing so, he says that Susan was so astonished by the openness of the craft beer industry that she excitedly invested in her son's idea of a craft brewery.

Bold City is currently available in twelve-pack bottles, six-pack cans, and on draft throughout Jacksonville, Saint Augustine, and Fernandina Beach with expansion into Tampa. The brewery's core beers are Killer Whale Cream Ale, Duke's Brown Ale, 1901 Red Ale, Mad Manatee IPA, and Archie's Rhino Rye Pale Ale. Since the Miller family are all native to Jacksonville, each beer has a tie to Jacksonville, the family, or the Jacksonville Zoo. Killer Whale is a family nickname for Brian, Duke was a boxer that Brian and his wife owned together, and 1901 was the year of the devastating Jacksonville Fire. Mad Manatee and Archie's Rhino both point to the Jacksonville Zoo, with which the brewery has a relationship.

The fruits of Bold City's family labor are poured at the tasting room in the front of the brewery. From the malty Duke's Brown ale to the not-a-red 1901 Red Ale combined with seasonals and occasionals, the tasting room combines the intimacy of a corner bar with the resources and ingenuity of a craft brewery, including an overflow bar into the brewery so that patrons do not have to wait for a pint if someone is filling growlers. The brewery will also throw in an occasional firkin to mix things up. The brewery brings in food trucks, hosts events and tournaments, and tries its best to engage the community in both beer and camaraderie on a regular basis.

Insider Tip: Bold City features the Jacksonville skyline on every label it produces.

Pinglehead Brewing (inside Brewer's Pizza)

Brewpub/Brewery
14B Blanding Boulevard, Orange Park 32073
(904) 276-5159
http://pinglehead.com
Closed Thursday

Pinglehead Brewing (and Brewer's Pizza that contains it) began as a small brewery, but like many Florida breweries quickly had trouble keeping up with demand. While currently designed as a brewpub, the owners have a vision of expanding production beyond just the friendly confines of Orange Park.

The pub itself is an archetypal pizzeria with a wooden bar in the middle. A large chalkboard displays the beers pouring currently,

and usually about six house offerings in addition to about nineteen other drafts from local brewers and national craft breweries. The typical draft runs about $4.50 and pairs well with the Italian fare of the pizzeria. The pizza crust is even infused with house beer.

The restaurant offers many forgotten traditions of past pubs, like a jukebox and skee ball, while there are plenty of televisions to enjoy sporting events, or for local pastimes like watching the Jaguars lose.

While the pub and brewery are both still young, and the core beers are still being decided, the most popular beers to date have been the sweet Pinglehead Red Ale, the citrusy Nine Voices IPA, and cocoa and hoppy Black HOPs Black IPA. These beers should be on draught for the long haul. Pinglehead is still working on its permanent lineup, but the Tribal Rite Oatmeal Stout looks like it might stick around as well. Pinglehead has also begun to tweak its standard lineup and add limited, specialty, and barrel-aged beers.

A trip during a special event might get a pour of Ghost Chili Mind Drive or Barrel Aged Ambitious Monk.

Look for Pinglehead to expand production and availability to more locations around Jacksonville, but for now Brewer's Pizza is perfecting a timeless combination in its favor: great beer and Italian food. After all, what's not to love about a brewery with a mascot like Pennywise the clown?

Green Room Brewing

Brewery
228 North 3rd Street, Jacksonville Beach 32250
(904) 201-9283
http://greenroombrewing.com
Closed Monday

Meandering down Jacksonville's beach road, A1A, yields several craft beer treasures along the shore. The first is Green Room Brewing. The beach air blows in many beer names from the sea shore, as well as patrons looking to slake their thirst. Situated within walking distance of several Jacksonville beaches, Green Room is taking craft beer to beachgoing tourists and locals alike.

The clean, well-lit tap room has a nice view of A1A with a small stage off to the side for live music. The bar takes up a good portion of the room, pouring seven or eight Green Room beers while graciously sharing space with several other Florida breweries on the tap list.

The brewery facility is actually located through a set of doors from the tap room. All of the brewing equipment is roped off from several picnic tables. Most of the brewery's property is usable by beer lovers for games like oversized Jenga or cornhole, or simply sitting to ponder one of Green Room's tasty beers. Picnic tables and outside air are usable, as is the ample tap room. Throughout Green Room is a sense of camaraderie with fellow beer enthusiasts.

Green Room's brewer, Eric Luman, began as a brewer at Jacksonville's Seven Bridges Grille and Brewery and engaged the locals there by sponsoring home brewers and perfecting his own recipes. In June of 2011 Green Room opened in its current space and began offering core beers of piney West Coast–style India pale ale called Head High IPA in addition to a grainy Munich helles lager called Helles Yeah. Later on in its history, Green Room's Pablo Beach Pale Ale was its first offering in cans. These beers are accompanied by the brewery's seasonals and occasional rarities.

Green Room's first anniversary beer (a bourbon barrel–aged imperial stout) perfectly describes the brewery, its location, and its beers. Its name? Secret Spot, although don't count on this beer haven to be a secret spot for very long with this much beer brewed mere feet from where it's served with live music and spirited conversation around a ping-pong table and patio rife with beach breezes.

Insider Tip: Green Room makes a single-hop, wet-hop series of beers called No Sticks, No Stems, No Seeds begun in September of 2013. Look for these IPAs to showcase the intense flavors of fresh hops (most hops are dried and pelletized; these hops are flown in fresh after picking).

Seven Bridges Grille and Brewery

Brewpub
9735 Gate Parkway North, Jacksonville 32246
(904) 997-1999
http://7bridgesgrille.com
Open 7 days a week

On the south side of Jacksonville, near many hotels and chain restaurants, lies Seven Bridges Grille and Brewery. On the outside, Seven Bridges looks like a standard restaurant with a brewery attached, but the beer is anything but standard. While the Gordon Biersch Brewery Restaurant Company owns Seven Bridges, the company allows leeway for its brewers to be creative and brew original beer for the restaurants as well.

Seven Bridges' brewery makes the usual suspects of a light pilsner, brown ale, IPA, and a token stout; brewer Aaron Nesbitt has two available taps at any given time to pour his beer next to Gordon Biersch's standard offerings. At the end of the draft tower, or maybe in a cask behind the bar, may be a vanilla stout or a bourbon barrel IPA made only for Seven Bridges by Nesbitt.

The brewery facilities are situated on a second story overlooking the restaurant. Aaron produces the restaurant's beer upstairs and pumps it to tanks downstairs to ferment, then into serving tanks so the restaurant can serve the beer directly from tanks situated several paces from the bar. The beer never sees a keg or other container, unless the brewery is attending an event.

While Seven Bridges may be owned by Gordon Biersch and may serve some of the same beers as other Gordon Biersch Restaurants, the offerings unique to Seven Bridges and some tasty beer and food pairings make this an excellent beer stop in Jacksonville.

Karibrew inside Café Karibo

Brewpub
27 North Third Street, Fernandina Beach 32034
(904) 277-5269
Open 7 days a week

Cozy Fernandina Beach is a small waterfront community that is like most coastal areas in Florida: a bit artsy and very popular at certain times of year. Fernandina Beach gets a bit cozy in terms of parking (think small community meets downtown parking) and the café is just off the main drag. Café Karibo is a well-lit, airy pub that serves generous portions and has beer made to satisfy patrons who want an icy pint with their meal. The interior is house-like and eclectic, with three large brite tanks right behind the bar from which the bartender serves the beer.

After I struck up a conversation with the bartender, he revealed that the beer is made on the premises, but that is a technical distinction. The wort is purchased from a brewery elsewhere and fermented in the large tanks behind the bar, where the beer is later poured into pints for patrons. The standard beers the house pours are the American Pilsner, Red Rocket Red Ale, Downtown Nut Brown, and Sloppy Skip's Stout. While the pilsner, red, and stout are all made, the Nut Brown is a blend of the pilsner and the stout. These seem to be readily available, as well as a summer wheat ale that appears as the mercury begins to soar.

Karibrew's beers are only available at the café, and are made to satisfy the thirst of the restaurant's patrons. In other words, if you are not a resident of Fernandina Beach, some travel is required.

A1A Ale Works

Brewpub
1 King Street, Saint Augustine 32084
(904) 829-2977
http://www.a1aaleworks.com
Open 7 days a week

A1A Ale Works, located on the waterfront in historic downtown Saint Augustine, with its wood and brass interior, is reminiscent of a bright and airy firehouse; if that firehouse also dished out

Floridian pub food and had taps flowing with craft beer. The glass windows at the end of the bar open onto the brewery, which when brewing radiates with the aroma of malted barley.

A1A Ale Works is owned by CraftWorks, and head brewer, Doug Murr, runs the brewing. Doug makes his beer on a ten-barrel system that runs against gravity. While most breweries that occupy several floors use the pull of the earth as a way to avoid having to pump beer around, A1A's bar is on the second floor, so serving the fresh beer requires beer to be pumped upstairs after fermenting downstairs. Space is tight in the brewery, but Doug makes it work; for many years A1A Ale Works was Saint Augustine's only craft brewery.

Like many of the other CraftWorks restaurants, A1A Ale Works keeps the taps stocked with corporate recipes and allows the brewer a few taps to play around with. A1A's standard beers are the light grain and floral hop King Street Light Lager, citrusy Porpoise Point IPA, a toasty Bridge of Lions Brown Ale, the malty Red Brick Ale, and the roasty A. Strange Stout (named for the founder's grandfather, not a statement about the beer). Here, Doug usually has two Brewer's Reserve taps on at any time; on my visit he had a Single Malt Pale Ale at 4.2 percent alcohol by volume with notes of tropical fruit and citrus, as well as a Strong Belgian Golden ale of 8.5 percent ABV with big notes of bubble gum, ripe banana, and fruit. Doug keeps his beers stocked for A1A's patrons—they range from tourists looking to try something and everything fresh to locals who have one beer and go home.

A1A Ale Works is a great place to stop for a bite and enjoy the ocean breeze off the Atlantic beaches while sipping on a fresh beer. Be warned about the parking: it's a downtown area and parking enforcement works quickly. Mind the parking signs, and just look for the overhanging signs to lead up the way to the Ale Works.

Insider Tip: Saint Augustine police monitor parking vigilantly in this area. Mind the signs, or risk of a parking ticket is high.

Mile Marker Brewing

Brewery
3420 Agricultural Center Dr., Suite 8, Saint Augustine 32092
(904) 217-4294
http://milemarkerbrewing.com
Closed Monday

Mile Marker Brewing is Saint Augustine's newest craft brewery and is keen on becoming a local brewery for anywhere in Florida. It is located in an industrial park just off I-95, but its beer is available

all the way down to Key West, which has proven to be its biggest market.

Mile Marker Brewing began in the most unlikely place for a Florida brewery: New Jersey. The idea for Mile Marker Brewing began December 5, 2008, when future brewer Vance Joy was at home enjoying the Christmas holiday, made a phone call to some friends, and suggested that they open a brewery. Originally, Vance was going to open a brewery in the Florida Keys, but the water and the price of real estate dissuaded him; instead he looked to Florida's oldest city: Saint Augustine. From there, the biggest challenge for Vance and his business partners was finding brewing equipment and a good spot. Because so many craft breweries are currently opening in the United States, any used brewing equipment is actually more expensive and sells faster than new equipment. Being a new brewer Mile Marker needed both space and equipment and did not want to break the bank. Serendipity struck one afternoon when Vance and company went to look at what would become their current 9,700-square-foot space: a set of brewing equipment was lying in storage on the spot. Apparently the equipment was the property of the defunct Hops Brewery and was discarded when the company disassembled its stores. The old Hops equipment was reborn as Mile Marker Brewing when Vance and company worked it into the lease. Mile Marker's diligence continued when they not only assembled the equipment but took the phrase "handcrafted" to a new level: much of the brewery, including the keg washer, bar, and some of the cold storage, was built by brewery staff.

The same work ethic that built the brewery has translated into the beer. Mile Marker has five core beers that are always on draft in the tasting room and are also sent into distribution. Mile Marker pours the light Mile Marker Zero Blonde Ale, the nutty and toasty Mile Marker 1513 Pecan de Leon Brown Ale, the malty Mile Marker 1565 Ancient City Red Ale, Mile Marker 70 Palm Beach Coconut Porter, and the citrusy Mile Marker 82 Islamorada IPA. Expect more rotating seasonals (including higher alcohol and bigger beers), additional canned beers, and increased expansion throughout Florida.

Mile Marker blends a dedication to quality and a dedication to the craft, and pours it out across Florida. Mile Marker's first priority is to the drinkability of its beers: Vance and his partners want to make their beers accessible in light of Florida's hot summers and mild winters.

Insider Tip: Look for Mile Marker 318 with Datil Peppers from time to time. Saint Augustine is the top producer of datil peppers in the world.

Ragtime Tavern

Brewpub
207 Atlantic Blvd., Atlantic Beach 32233
(904) 241-7877
http://ragtimetavern.com
Open 7 days a week

Ragtime Tavern is the brewpub that serves the tourists and locals of Jacksonville Beach and Atlantic Beach. Ragtime also stands as one of Florida's oldest continuously operating brewpubs; 2013 marked its twentieth anniversary of brewing and the thirtieth anniversary of the brewpub.

Ragtime is yet another key brewpub in the keychain of Craft-Works brewpubs, and like A1A Ale Works, allows for the sampling of fresh beer near the same Atlantic breezes—it's right off the beach. Brewer Scott Bannester brews Ragtime's beers and uses the

ten-barrel brewing system to its fullest potential. Ragtime began in 1993 and was originally owned by the Morton family, as was A1A Ale Works, and Seven Bridges was going to be the family's next investment. The Big River Restaurant chain then came in and bought the restaurants and was allowed to use the name of the Gordon Biersch restaurants; at that point Gordon Biersch's beers were not currently distributed in Florida. Then a new company was formed, CraftWorks, and it bought Ragtime Tavern, A1A Ale Works, and Seven Bridges Grille and Brewery; this also brought a new infusion of capital and ideas to Ragtime.

Ragtime has four flagship beers on at all times in addition to one rotating seasonal beer and one brewer's choice beer. Ragtime will always have on its core beers: Dolphin's Breath Lager breathes lightest, followed by the caramel-sweet Red Brick Ale, the slightly cocoa-flavored Sweet Magnolia Brown, and the heavy-breathing A. Strange Stout.

Ragtime has endured for a while, and after undergoing renovations in the summer of 2013 is looking as good as ever. Ragtime is part of the community of fresh beers being made along Jacksonville Beach.

Engine 15 Brewing Company

Brewery/Brewpub
1500 Beach Blvd., Jacksonville Beach 32250
(904) 249-2337
http://engine15.com
Open 7 days a week

Engine 15 is a craft beer gem in the tiara of Jacksonville's beach area. Engine 15 stands in a nondescript strip mall off eastbound Beach Boulevard. It is easily spotted in the daytime because of the presence of its namesake: the 1962 Ford C100 fire engine in the furthest parking space.

There was an Engine 15 long before there was an Engine 15 Brewing Company. When brewer Luciano Scremin was a college freshman he became a home brewer and began to love beer. After much work, his career in the airline industry allowed him to travel the world and sample all manner of beer styles. Then Luciano, who is called Luch by his friends, would travel around Jacksonville in his fire engine and tailgate or hang out with friends. "Engine 15" became synonymous with good friends, cherished memories, and admirable beers. When it came time to name the brewery and pub, there was no choice in a name and Engine 15 Brewing Company was born. The brewery began as a brewpub and has since expanded its licensing to include growler sales. It has doubled in size since opening in July of 2010 and embarking on brewing operations in July of 2012.

Engine 15's beers are available in distribution around Florida. Engine 15 focuses most on experimenting with flavors and ingredients in the beers and educating the community about artisanal beer. The pub also has over sixty taps, with about ten of those usually filled with Engine 15 beer, including Tap 42, which the brewery staff fills with a never-before-seen beer every Thursday. Engine 15 has six core beers that it works to keep on draft and send to distribution. This family of beers lists Route 90 Session IPA, weighing in at 4.8 percent alcohol; Double Nut Sack Brown Ale, a double nut brown ale at 7 percent alcohol; the citrus hoppy Old Battle Axe IPA; the Doolittle Rye Saison getting stronger at 8.5 percent alcohol; Rye of the Tiger, a rye pale ale that uses rye to bring out some spicy notes; and a 4.7 percent hefeweizen called 904 Weissguy. Engine 15 also rotates through numerous seasonals including the not-to-be-missed Citra wet hop pale ale.

Engine 15 also takes community education to a new level as it allows the public, for a fee, to come in and brew their own beer with established recipes from Engine 15. The brewing staff will help prospective brewers by walking them through the process of brewing, fermenting, and packaging the beer, leading to greater understanding of the finished beer.

Engine 15's founding principles are the beginnings of any great beer: good friends, good memories, and enjoyable beer. Look to Engine 15 to keep evolving and growing across the Sunshine State, especially after the opening of the brewery's production facility on Myrtle Avenue in Jacksonville.

Insider Tip: Every Christmas, Engine 15 brews the 12 Beers of Christmas where twelve different beers are tapped in twelve successive days in the taproom.

River City Brewing Company

Brewpub
835 Museum Circle, Jacksonville 32207
(904) 398-2299
http://rivercitybrew.com
Open 7 days a week

River City Brewing Company is a scenic seafood pub on the waterfront near downtown Jacksonville. The beers are consistent in their production with occasional seasonal beers joining the lineup. The brewery stands adjacent to the Jacksonville Friendship Fountain and looks out at a stunning view of the St. Johns River.

River City Brewing Company began brewing in 1993 and uses all German two-row malted barley and hops from Washington and Oregon. The system used to make the beer sits behind the bar and is visible from the bar area.

River City Brewing Company has a standard four core beers that are on draft almost constantly and it cycles through a limited list of seasonals, which in the past have included a spiced ale during the Christmas season, a wheat ale during the scorching summer months, and an Oktoberfest during the traditional September/October months. The core four include the mild Jag Light; Jackson Pale Ale, a pale ale brewed with citrusy hops; Red Rooster Ale, a mildly malty red ale; and Riptide Porter, a mildly roasty dark ale. Look to River City for seafood and an ale on the water.

River City Brewing Company offers probably the most wide-open parking situation of any brewery in the state of Florida and a view of the St. Johns that allows for beer and conversation.

Aardwolf Brewing Company

Brewery
1461 Hendricks Ave., Jacksonville 32207
(904) 301-0755
http://www.aardwolfbrewing.com
Closed Monday and Tuesday

Aardwolf Brewing Company has been a name in Florida brewing for many years with Jacksonvillians asking owner Preben Olsen "what's up with the brewery" for a while. Ultimately Aardwolf ended up in a renovated ice factory, the former home of the Jacksonville Ice Company, and spent a plethora of time and effort searching the proverbial woods like Little Red Riding Hood, seeking the perfect home for the Aardwolf.

Aardwolf began licensing and applying to become a brewery around 2008, the same time that Cigar City Brewing was going through the same process. With delays, construction, and time, by the time Aardwolf opened and began brewing beer, it was one of Florida's most anticipated breweries. Aardwolf first opened as a bar, then opened as a tap room on a limited basis as most beers were brewed on a ten-gallon pilot system. Finally, in August of 2013, Aardwolf began brewing on its fifteen-barrel commercial system. The staff had the patience of wolves waiting for the brewery, named after the English translation for *Humulus lupulus*, or hop plant, to materialize, but when the stars aligned, the beers that issued from it would intrigue even Romulus and Remus.

Aardwolf has four core beers that it brews on a large scale, but with its pilot system well established, it will continue to brew small batches and circulate recipes to see what the Jacksonville craft beer community enjoys. Aardwolf's core beers are the hoppy and light Nonchalant Session IPA; the citrusy, banana, and fruity Belgian Pale Ale; the 7 percent alcohol, roasty and citrusy Eastbound and

Brown; and finally a dark chocolate and roasted malt stout called Styrofoam Pony. As for the pilot system, it is a blank canvas. The beers that have come from Aardwolf's pilot system so far include a mango Berliner weiss for 2013 Berliner Bash and several sour beers for Ratebeer Winter Gathering 2013 that displayed the depths of Aardwolf brewer Michael Payne's abilities.

Aardwolf is a fixture in South Jacksonville. Owner, brewer, and staff have transformed their space from a dirt-floored historic building into a craft brewery that melds the descriptors "modern" and "comfortable" yet displays a vintage and historic feel at the same time.

Insider Tip: Many of Aardwolf's beers are produced on a small pilot system. Look for releases like coffee stout, guava lactic zepplin, and Galactus devourer of hops double IPA to be drafted from the pilot system.

Tomoka Brewery

Brewpub
188 East Granada Boulevard, Ormond Beach 32176
(386) 673-6777
http://www.tomokabrewery.com
Closed Tuesday

Tomoka Brewery is the result of trained pastry chef Peter Szunyogh and his wife, pizza shop veteran Jennifer Hawkins, discovering the home brewing hobby together. After about a year of home brewing, the couple considered opening a pub in several cities in Florida. After deciding on the Tomoka area of Ormond Beach (near Daytona), the couple found a space and signed the papers, and posted their first Facebook photos of the place on April 20, 2013. The small pub opened to its first customers in July, electing to open as a pub and craft beer bar while waiting on federal approval for its brewing permits.

Tomoka Brewery has recipes for all manner of beers, but the one that became the most talked about was Elvis's Peanut Butter and Banana Sandwich Brown Ale. Weighing in at 5.9 percent alcohol, this beer is meant to mimic the flavors in the King of Rock and Roll's favorite sandwiches. Aside from Elvis's ale, Jennifer and Peter also brew Orange Blossom Special, a hefeweizen; Southern Iced Tea Red IPA; and Pumpernickel Bread Porter.

Tomoka Brewery's space is very limited, so Peter and Jennifer settled on a one-barrel brewing system for the pub and began looking for space nearby to house a 3–5-barrel production system. Look for Tomoka brews at Tomoka Brewery until that new space and new brewing system are secured.

Swamp Head Brewery

Brewery
3140 Southwest 42nd Way, Gainesville 32608
(352) 505-3035
http://swamphead.com
Closed Monday; tours offered Tuesday

Situated off the busy roads of the city that boasts national champion NCAA sports teams and one of the largest public universities in Florida, in the quiet of a few cypress trees, resides Gainesville's Swamp Head Brewery. Adjacent to the brewery is The Wetlands, Swamp Head's wooden-themed tasting room that shows off both current and future projects that Swamp Head is working on.

Owner Luke Kemper is a native of Gainesville who spotted a keg-shaped hole in Gainesville's beer market. Upon graduation from the University of Colorado, Luke began developing a business plan to open a brewery in his hometown and enlisted the help of accomplished brewer Craig Birkmaier. Luke and Craig currently work to make Swamp Head beer for Florida markets, distributing their beer

from Vero Beach to Fort Myers and north to Tallahassee. Swamp Head Brewery opened in 2010 and has faced a steady increase in demand from its thirsty home base of Gainesville. Swamp Head is currently expanding its production capacity to meet demand for the entirety of the Sunshine State. Swamp Head and its beers are a tribute to what a small group of passionate people can do. Swamp Head's success is proof—Swamp Head runs its entire operation with six core employees. Those six employees tripled the amount of beer sold in one year (700 bbls in 2010 to 2,100 bbls in 2011). Swamp Head's rapid growth and strange fortune have given them cause to search for a new facility, and they are building a new brewery from the ground up.

Swamp Head has five beers in the Year-Round Fleet. Swamp Head's beers begin with very light Wild Night Cream Ale, which adds a touch of honey to a light malt profile, and go to Cottonmouth, a slightly fruity Belgian-style wheat beer. The bigger beers from the Swamp start with a hoppy pale ale, Stumpknocker, move to the aromatic and citrusy Big Nose IPA, and finish with a coffee-forward stout, dubbed Midnight Oil. Swamp Head also moved to start making more seasonal ales in its Migrational Series, beginning with an Irish Red ale, a Blonde ale, a saison, and a spiced Belgian wheat beer.

A GPS or a sharp eye will help to spot 42nd Way, but the rewards for doing so are great. The brewery is situated off the beaten path, but the tasting room has Swamp Head beers that are not available anywhere else (as the brewery has installed a small pilot brewing system), Swamp Head regular beers, and some guest beers from around Florida.

Insider Tip: Keep an eye out when inside Swamp Head; its copper-jacketed brewing vessels are from the Spanish Springs Brewing Company, a historic Florida brewery and one special to Birkmaier.

Alligator Brewing (inside Tall Paul's Ale House)

Brewery
10 Southeast 2nd Avenue, Gainesville 32601
(352) 505-0990
http://alligatorbrewing.com
Open 7 days a week

At the front of the historic building on 2nd Avenue in downtown Gainesville, Tall Paul's coat of arms sticks out, as does its namesake upon entering the bar—owner Paul is gifted with great height. Nestled into a niche of downtown Gainesville, Tall Paul's is a craft beer hamlet.

The owner, Paul, was a sales representative for Shipyard brewing before lighting out on his own to pursue his craft beer ambitions. Along with brewer, Neal Mackowiak, the two are creating beers that blur the lines of style and create unique taste profiles. Alliga-

tor Brewing has made over forty different types of beer since opening in 2011. The most popular styles so far have been Alligator Pale
Ale and a Black Rye IPA, so their return might be imminent. Other
style-bending beers include a brown wheat porter, a mango red ale,
and a ginger sour ale.

The bar itself is open with a few tables and an open space in
the rear for live music. Tall Paul's usual crowd features graduate
students and young professionals, with plenty of friendly people to
talk about the beer. The bar runs with several dozen taps, trying at
all times to keep four house beers on draft. So far Alligator Brewing
has not identified its core brand of beers. Paul and Neal want to
keep rotating the house beers they offer—both for variety and to
see what the good people of Gainesville prefer.

The on-site brewery facility is relatively small, a thirty-gallon system, but both owner and brewer have big dreams. One day, several years from now, they would like to rival cross-town production brewery Swamp Head in size and scope.

BREWERIES IN FERMENTATION

Persimmon Hollow Brewing Company

Persimmon Hollow is a future brewery in the DeLand area. Andie Sistrunk and Robbie Carelli are home brewers who are seeking their shot at the dream of brewing craft beers and ciders using locally sourced ingredients and creating a community space. The pair received a community redevelopment grant from the city of DeLand to help with renovations of their chosen space and secured financing for their project.

First Magnitude Brewing Company

Beer lovers of Gainesville are awaiting the opening of First Magnitude Brewing Company, named after Florida's first magnitude springs. Construction of the fifteen-barrel brewery system and tap room is nearly complete, and the brewery will feature three year-round beers, Siren blonde ale, 72° pale ale, and Drift English Mild, in addition other innovative offerings.

Beer in the Panhandle

Brewing in Florida's Northwest

NORTHWEST FLORIDA'S BREWING PAST

Like Jacksonville before, Pensacola had one man who was brave enough to declare his intention to make beer in the years preceding national Prohibition. One brave soul yelled out into the blackness of history that he was going to make beer. His name was Lewis Klein of Tampa and the year was 1902. The name of the proposed brewery was lost to the unkindness of history and the economic downturn that Pensacola faced after an abysmal hurricane in the same year. Pensacola's difficult economic fortunes proved unfriendly to many businesses until relief came in the form of a government installation that would grow to become synonymous with the blossoming North Florida city on the gulf.

When the Naval Aeronautical Flight School (and subsequent Naval Air Station) was built in Pensacola in 1914, it caused a massive upturn in spending and an even bigger planting of families and soldiers into the northwest coast of Florida. That emerging economy drew several kindred spirits to invest in the Crystal Ice Company in 1929, but these men had their eyes on bigger and better investments in the City of Five Flags. That same year one of the main investors, Guy Spearman, journeyed to Monterrey, Mexico, to investigate the beer and brewing techniques of a brewery there. Spearman thought the time was right to open a brewery in Pensacola for three reasons: first, the closest brewery to Pensacola would have been in Mobile, Alabama, or Jacksonville, Florida. He could save on shipping costs and just supply the local market, which consisted of thousands of new residents, thanks to the Naval Station. Second, with the repeal of the Prohibition of the Eighteenth Amendment, breweries across the country were opening their doors to slake the thirst of deprived beer drinkers. Finally, Spearman was already an investor in an ice company, so not only was the existing company profitable, but there would be capital and supplies to help support the new operation. Opening a brewery could be like searching for a second job when the first one is still paying well: a possible win-win situation.

After considering options, Spearman and several fellow investors opened the Gulf Brewing Company in 1933. The venture began well, but after a short stint Spearman decided to withdraw from the partnership because the partners wanted to use second-hand equipment and Spearman did not agree with that practice. In May 1933, Spearman got involved with the local Budweiser and Schlitz distributorship in order to stay in the beer business. Still, a part of the business did not sit well with Spearman, so in 1934, he announced his intentions to the brewing world, via Western Brewer Magazine, to open his own brewery.

Spearman and his fellow investors broke ground on a new facility at Barrancas Avenue at I Street in Pensacola. The first order of business for the brewery was to obtain the purest water available. Spearman ordered a well dug to retrieve that water; it reached 300 feet into the ground and retrieved water that tested 99.993 percent pure, and a Layne pump brought up to 1,000 gallons per minute

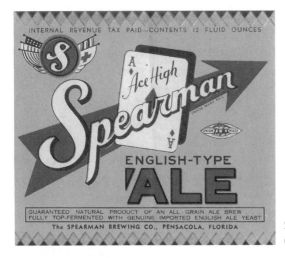

Spearman Ale poster.
Courtesy of Michael Zane.

from the well. From the beginning, the water was one of Spearman's talking points. He claimed that the pure water and a system he designed to reintroduce carbon dioxide into his beer imparted a carbonated and foamy character that made the beer so tasty.

In an artist's rendition shared by Spearman's descendants with beer researcher Kip Sharpe, Spearman had the building designed with a seventy-five-barrel brew kettle, a two-story stock house with eighty-barrel wooden fermentation tanks, and a bottle house that could bottle forty barrels of beer in one day. As a nod to the unstable nature of Pensacola's hurricane seasons, a steel skeleton was built to reinforce the brewery's structure; the brewery could and would withstand light breezes and blinding gales in the same day.

From the beginning, local residents, both military and civilian, seemed to enjoy the beer. The same year the brewery opened, restrictions were lifted on the strength of beer in the southernmost state. Spearman Brewing Company took advantage of the removal and began brewing some pretty strong beers for the 1930s. While other breweries around the state would boast beers with 6 and 7 percent alcohol by volume, Spearman canned "Strate Eight" among the first brands. Since advertising a beer's alcohol content was prohibited, many times brewers would work the beer's alcohol content into the beer's brand name. Strate Eight was so successful that it would be canned and sold for over twenty years. Strate Eight powered the brewery through its first expansion when the brewery increased its capacity to 110,000 barrels annually.

Then World War II hit and military spending brought new money to Pensacola, but war rationing looked to hurt the brewery by limiting ingredients and resources. The war rationing mandated that Spearman use 20 percent less ingredients to produce the same amount of beer, but the great business allowed for Spearman to hire more workers, increasing brewery staff threefold from 50 employees to 150. As Spearman's son recalled, Spearman was a stickler for quality and a marketing prodigy, and was able to fill in some brewery resources (like metal and raw materials) by purchasing them through the ice works, since the ice works was considered a more necessary business.

Once the war was in full swing, and the military personnel made their presence felt, Spearman's ledgers could not move fast enough to record the profits. Sales increased steadily in the early 1940s and in 1943 brought Spearman's heaviest volume sold in a year—80,000 barrels. Sailors would report going to the brewery on a Sunday to get beer after a tour and the brewery would be dry. If the locals went through fifty kegs on a Friday and Saturday, Spearman would simply make more beer. The problem was that the locals were drinking as fast as the brewery could make the beer. At its peak, the locals were drinking seventy kegs of Spearman beer in one weekend (before Sunday). Assuming that Spearman made beer in standard half-barrel kegs, then 35 barrels or almost 1,100 gallons of beer were consumed in two days, on any given weekend. While those days would not last, it would have been difficult to convince a weekend Spearman bartender of this fact.

If the years of World War II were the height of Spearman's business, then the darkest days lay ahead, as they did for all breweries in Florida and America. In 1948, Spearman's sales plummeted from the usual 80,000 barrels to 42,000 barrels. The brewery's answer: get the word out. The brewery spent over $100,000 each year on advertising. Brewery staff would push promotional materials, and Spearman worked on getting beer into as many coolers as possible. He would label each can "Keep Beer Cold." While the beer would not spoil if it warmed to room temperature, it either made the retailer think that it could spoil, or even better, made the consumer ask for it in the cooler. This pushed possible competitors out of that cooler shelf space and into the less popular warm spaces of the beer stores. Spearman proved his marketing acumen with his attention to details like these.

After the slip in sales, the Spearman Brewery's governing board, especially the widow of Spearman's original partner, decided they wanted new leadership. B. F. Jenkins was that new president, and he introduced new brands like Viking and bon to the market. After a disastrous year in 1951, Guy Spearman was asked to resume his presidency in 1952. As Guy Spearman Jr. recalls it, Mr. Jenkins "almost ruined the company." With Jenkins's new brands, the brewery toiled to remain current in brewing and bottling technology. In 1952, Spearman's return heralded a call for modernization—a new bottling line (the outmoded line could package 160 cans per minute) and eight new tanks to raise annual capacity to 120,000 barrels.

The tailspin the company began after World War II continued despite large expenditures on advertising and modernizing. Continuing pressure from his partner's widow and increasing red margins finally caused Spearman to sell the brewery to the Hertzberg Foundation in 1960. The Spearman family remained in business with the ice works, but ceased ownership of the brewery. In 1964, the Hertzberg Foundation ceased all North American operations and sold all of its holdings on the continent in hopes of pursuing the brewing business elsewhere.

Pensacola would remain without a local craft brewery for many decades, until enterprising and beer-loving friends joined together in the positive craft beer climate of the late 1980s. McGuire's two locations in northwest Florida helped pave the way for craft beer in the panhandle, along with Tallahassee's Buckhead Brewpub. The Mill Restaurant and Brewery of Orlando also made several forays into Florida's panhandle and beyond into Alabama. Those breweries all went under during the rough economic seas around the year 2000. It was not until Proof Brewing and Fermentation Lounge joined Florida's panhandle breweries that McGuire's got any company in the touristy areas between Florida's capital and Alabama. The panhandle continues to expand with the unprecedented and continuous addition of breweries and brewpubs.

NORTHWEST FLORIDA'S BREWING PRESENT

McGuire's Irish Pub and Brewery (two locations)

Brewpub
600 East Gregory St., Pensacola 32502
(850) 433-6789

33 Highway 98, Destin 32541
(850) 650-0000
http://mcguiresirishpub.com
Open 7 days a week

McGuire's Irish Pub and Brewery has two locations, one in Destin and one in Pensacola. The location in Destin looks like a leprechaun-themed amusement park, and the location in Pensacola

looks like a leprechaun's summer cottage. Both locations are attractive and verdant outside and papered with dollar bills and undergarments on the inside. McGuire's motto is "Feasting, Imbibery, and Debauchery," and the interior has the welcoming feel of the place your mother always warned you about. The servers dress as Ireland's finest, and each location makes its own beer.

McGuire's is Florida's oldest operating brewpub, having opened the first location in Pensacola in 1977. After outgrowing its space, the landmark pub moved to its current space in Pensacola in 1987 and added the attached brewery. In 1987, McGuire's opened its second location in the beach destination of Destin. Each location is currently making its own beer to serve on site. McGuire's of Destin is still using the original equipment to brew on, so a bit of McGuire's history is brewed into every pint. The brewpub has reached capacity in terms of production, so the brewpub is currently looking into options for expanding brewing operations.

McGuire's is one of Florida's craft beer old-timers, and its beer recipes have been perfected by brewers and praised by patrons and critics alike. McGuire's is one of the few places that can boast that it was visited by the venerable beer writer Michael Jackson (the British beer journalist, not the singer). He commented on the quality of the Irish red ale and the uniqueness of the place in his *Pocket Guide to Beer* and other books. While McGuire's still brews the Irish red that Michael Jackson drank and praised, it brews other notable beers and serves up pub grub in herculean portions. One of the most impressive features of McGuire's regular lineup of beers is how flavorful they are while they contain mild to moderate amounts of alcohol. McGuire's roasty cream stout has a nice body and notes of chocolate and some light coffee bitterness. Put side-by-side with a certain other Irish-style stout with a much larger advertising budget, McGuire's stout will shine like Irish Eyes—and a bit heftier too at 5.2 percent alcohol. Not to be outdone, McGuire's porter closes the books at 5.3 percent alcohol and contains a hefty dose of chocolate and earth but will allow for conversation with friends and peers alike. Not to be confined to darker styles, McGuires also serves a raspberry wheat beer (4.8 percent ABV) and an old-fashioned ale (4.2 percent ABV) for those who seek lighter beers. Finally, for the seeker of bigger and bolder beers, there is a rotating seasonal that could include an imperial stout, scotch ale, or an imperial apricot IPA.

The bottom line here is that McGuire's is the Disney World of Florida beer. When visiting Orlando with the children, one must visit that institution. When visiting Destin or Pensacola, adults must visit this institution. After all, it's Florida's oldest existing brewery.

Insider Tip: Beware the bathrooms at McGuire's. Read the signs on the door or just watch the gender of the person coming out. Simply scanning the sign will result in your going to the opposite sex's bathroom.

Pensacola Bay Brewery

Brewery
225 East Zaragoza St., Pensacola 32502
(850) 434-3353
http://pbbrew.com
Open 7 days a week

Pensacola Bay is one of Florida's up-and-coming breweries. This small brewery is currently Florida's westernmost brewery and sets its clocks by the central time zone. It has a bright, airy, open, nautical-themed tasting room in the heart of a waterside historical district in Pensacola. The locals certainly know about this brewery, as there is a steady stream of people flowing through the door looking to fill a growler or to stay for a pour.

Pensacola Bay Brewery's website boasts that "Once upon a time, two guys who had never met had a glass of beer. Who knew that years later, their love of beer would bring them together." Brewery

owners Mark Robertson and Elliot Eckland decided to go into business together making and distributing beer for the City of Five Flags and the whole Sunshine State, if possible. Pensacola Bay Brewery opened in October of 2010 and grew to produce over 14,000 barrels of beer in its first full year in business. The owners moved to double that production in 2012. The brewery has produced enough beer to move down the west coast of Florida, and distribution on Florida's east coast followed suit. Pensacola Bay's story is the story of what dedication and a mutual love of beer can produce. The owners met as strangers and now co-own a successful business.

Pensacola Bay's story is written every day in liquid ink: the brewery's nautical-themed tasting room has fourteen tap lines, usually with several nonalcoholic offerings atop its list. Aside from root beer and cream soda, the brewery's core lineup includes a citrus-forward IPA (Lil' Napoleon®), a light and hoppy kolsch-style ale (DeLuna extra pale ale), a malty and sweet amber (Riptide amber ale), a roasty chocolaty porter (Lighthouse porter), a spicy and somewhat earthy brown ale (Banyan brown ale), and an earthy yet smooth oatmeal stout named for a commensurately dark soul (Blackbeard oatmeal stout). Seasonal offerings from this West Florida craft brewery include a pale ale brewed with citra hops (called Treasure Grove), a light and sweet pilsner (1845 pilsner), a wheat ale named for the ubiquitous Florida greenery (Sawgrass wheat), a somewhat biscuity ESB (named simply Pensacola Bay's ESB), a fall favorite dessert beer (Vanilla Pumpkin Porter), a malty doppelbock (Conquistador), and a light and tart wheat beer with raspberries for the blazing summer months (DeSoto Berliner Weisse Ale).

All points in the Sunshine State will see Pensacola Bay's beers on the horizon. The brewery's expansion in late 2012 saw increased capacity and a nascent barrel-aging program (with the addition of a Jack Daniels–aged porter called Black Treasure Porter). More space and more production led Pensacola Bay forward—from the westernmost point of Florida, the brewery eyes the southernmost point and beyond.

Insider Tip: A day trip to Pensacola Bay Brewery will require changing time zones. Remember that most of Florida may be in the eastern time zone, but PBB is on central time.

Grayton Beer Company

Brewery
217 Serenoa Road, Santa Rosa Beach 32461
(850) 231-4786
http://graytonbeer.com/

Grayton Beer Company began the craft beer journey as a contract brewery, just producing bottles for sale in local shops and kegs for local bars. When fate struck, the time was right for Grayton to progress into its own production brewery, and progress it did—from contracting to building a 30,000-square-foot brewery directly off U.S. 98 in Fort Walton.

Grayton is run by owner Jamey Price and brewer Brad Shankweiler, who began the entire operation with a pale ale and an IPA. Price and Shankweiler first had to educate consumers in an area with many temporary beach residents. They did this by pouring their beer at various festivals and gatherings throughout the panhandle.

Grayton Brewing Company is currently expanding beyond the two beers originally contract brewed at Florida Beer Company. The originals, Grayton Pale Ale is a light and somewhat citrusy, easy-drinking pale ale while the Grayton IPA tends a bit more toward the hop-assertive with some grapefruit notes coming out to play in the beer. Grayton has expanded its lineup, and as brewery building comes to a close, the journey from contract beer to production brewery has been a three-year trip.

Grayton Pale Ale and IPA are currently available in Florida's panhandle, from Fort Walton Beach to Apalachicola. With the addition of a large brewing system, Grayton has plans to expand southeastward, looking to grow into Florida's thirsty craft beer market.

Idyll Hounds Brewing Company

Brewery
845 Serenoa Road, Santa Rosa Beach 32459
(850) 231-1138
http://www.idyllhoundsbrewingcompany.com

Idyll Hounds Brewing Company is the child of two chefs who met in the kitchen of a Rosemary Beach restaurant in 2011. When founders Frasier Hansen and Shawn Sherman began enjoying beers together, they did not foresee their passion becoming a brewery, until it did.

As fate would have it, Idyll Hounds became closer to reality when Frasier began working in a home brew shop after moving to Utah. After becoming a skilled home brewer, he decided to look into furthering his beer making skills, so he looked into going to brewing school. As American brewing schools have a two-year waiting list, he looked into a beer education in England. Frasier was accepted to Brewlab in the United Kingdom and was able to work with skilled and accomplished British brewers in crafting masterful beers. Upon returning to the United States, Frasier was anxious to put those skills to work and open a brewery with Sherman. The startup still needed a little help, and the brewery's namesake stepped in. Frasier's parents offered to help fund the project, and since Frasier's father was nicknamed "the Hound," it seemed only fitting to include "Hound" in the name. Upon searching for adjectives, the two found that idyll described their ideal, thus Idyll Hounds sprang into being.

Idyll Hounds Brewing Company shines as the newest addition to the Emerald Coast's community of brewers. The brewery is making its name with two core beers, as seasonals and rotating beers are under development. The 8 percent hoppy double IPA Divide and Conch'r will be the first flagship, a trophy for hop heads followed by 4 percent Man O'Wheat, an unfiltered wheat beer for slaking a Florida thirst.

Idyll Hounds will be anything but idle, as Frasier and Shawn work toward their production goal of 2,000 barrels in their first year, both in cans and kegs. As they seek to grow with demand into new markets, look for Idyll Hounds to be available closer to its panhandle home, at least at first.

Uncle Ernie's Bayfront Grill

Contract Brew Brewpub
1151 Bayview Avenue, Panama City 32401
(850) 763-8427
http://uncleerniesbayfrontgrill.com
Closed Monday

Uncle Ernie's Bayfront Grill is a place to watch the sun set over Saint Andrew's Bay in Panama City. While the restaurant does not contain the brewery, as the beer is brewed off-premises at Sweetwater Brewing Company in Atlanta, the environment for consuming the beer is Panama City exclusive.

Uncle Ernie's decided in 2012 to add craft beers to its menu, since beers and bays seem made for one another. Uncle Ernie's has three specific beers made exclusively for the restaurant: Miss Jessie's Light Blue Brew, Uncle Ernie's Amber Ale, and Inne's Pale Ale. Miss Jessie's is aimed at those who seek the fruit and the fun of having a beer but can do without the full body of an ale; it's a light lager with a hint of blueberry. Uncle Ernie's Amber Ale is for the more beer-minded folks: it is malty with a touch of hops. The amber is bitter enough to drink by itself and not overpowering, and it can still pair with some of the foods on Ernie's menu. Finally, Inne's Pale Ale is on the lighter side of hoppy—while the menu simply says that it is full-bodied and complex, the beer drinker will see a touch of hops and a malt character that could possibly enhance a catch of the day or possibly an ahi tuna. Uncle Ernie's three core beers are available solely on premises at Uncle Ernie's Bayfront Grill.

Props Brewery and Grill

Brewpub
225 Miracle Strip Parkway Southeast, Fort Walton Beach 32548
(850) 586-7117
http://propsbrewery.com
Open 7 days a week

Props Brewery and Grill serves the military population of the Pensacola/Destin area while also catering to the tourists of West Florida's beaches. This bright pub serves food and beer to a diverse clientele with a telling sign on the wall: "In wine there is truth, in beer there is strength, in water there is bacteria . . ." At Props, strength is served by the pint.

Props is the product of a military education in beer. The owners serve in the United States Air Force as C130 pilots and balance their military careers with business ownership and brewing beer. The brewery and pub divides its attention between aviation and beer—the brewing equipment takes up a portion of the pub floor, but it is kept cool by the pub fan: a 330-pound DC3 propeller circulates the smell of seafood and malted barley throughout the welcoming establishment. The story of Props starts with servicemen and women who served in duty stations around the world and in the process rotated through fine brewing countries like Germany and the United Kingdom. Ninety percent of these men and women develop a thirst for the type of beers made in these overseas duty stations. While the Panama City or Valparaiso areas of Florida have breweries, the existing ones may not make the type of beers that

the service members have grown accustomed to. This is where the notion for Props began: to serve German-influenced beers that the military personnel thirsted for while they served in a West Florida duty station.

Props has been open since December 16, 2011, and brewing operations began May 1, 2012. Props serves three core beers at all times: a blonde ale, a brown ale, and an IPA. The blonde ale is a nice introduction to craft beer while the earthy brown ale and IPA are a bit more appealing to the craft beer drinker; they are still very approachable. With the success and acceptance of its core lineup, Props also works together a few seasonal ales beginning with a pumpkin ale and a chocolate porter. The next step in its craft beer journey was to upgrade its licensure to include growlers, and next is possibly an off-site brewery down the road.

Props's concept is a simple one that has worked for many breweries and brewpubs around the country: make tasty and approachable beers in a laid-back atmosphere with a local theme and make a mark in the community. It has done just that in a short time in business and has continued its ascent until reaching a comfortable cruising altitude.

Insider Tip: Props is a great place to try unique house beers, but it also strives (like many Florida breweries) to carry beer from comrade panhandle breweries.

Momo's Pizza and Brew

Brewpub (two locations but Market Street has the brewery)
1410 Market Street, Tallahassee 32312
(850) 412-0222
http://momospizza.com
Open 7 days a week

The Tallahassee pizza restaurant with "slices as big as your head!" has its own beer. Someone long ago decided that pizza and beer made the perfect marriage, and at Momo's that marriage is celebrated by the freshness of both the food and the beer.

Momo's Pizza and Brew is also the offspring of the friendship between Momo's owner Donny Dye and John Larsen, the owner of a local home brew shop, The Homebrew Den, and a certified beer judge. The restaurant itself opened in 1999 on Tennessee Street and added another location where Donny ran a small catering kitchen. Momo's Pizza on Market Street then decided to cool the catering ovens, and Donny contacted John Larsen and told him if he ever wanted to brew professionally, "now is the time." That was in September of 2011; Donny and John never looked back, and forty batches and several medals in Florida beer competitions later, Larsen's beer continues pouring at Momo's on Market Street. Momo's primary goal is to introduce people to craft beer and show

them that it is accessible to all. To that end, Momo's brews what Donny describes as "full-bodied beers." Momo's favors IPAs, stouts, and brown ales that are appealing to many, not simply beers with extreme amounts of alcohol.

Like many other breweries and brewpubs around Florida, Momo's claims no real core beers, merely beers that come around the rotation wheel faster. The most popular beer at Momo's is the aggressively hoppy Hopnosis Double IPA, followed closely by Otis IPA, Hopnosis's younger cousin. The nutty Moose and Squirrel Double Brown Ale follow after that in terms of popularity. Larsen, who is a professor at nearby Florida State University during his daytime hours, continues to pour at Momo's, assisted by his wife, Sarah Bridegroom. The business has no real interest in expanding brewing operations very far, save maybe to the other Momo's location across Tallahassee, and possibly canning or bottling its beer in the distant future. As the local response to Momo's has been great, the restaurant trusts its loyal customers to spread the word about the beer and the business.

In a town with only a few craft breweries, Momo's is Tallahassee's only brewpub. Look for Momo's at the Tallahassee beer festivals, or on draft in its own house with a massive slice of pie.

Golden Horn Brewing inside Fermentation Lounge

Brew Bar/Brewery
113 All Saints St., Tallahassee 32301
(850) 727-4033
http://fermentationlounge.com
Open 7 days a week

The Fermentation Lounge is one of the most unusual places in this book in many ways. This cozy spot is located in the basement of an apartment building; when GPS monitors are unable to find the address, that is why. Cruising down All Saints Street in Tallahassee, the lounge, or "The Ferm" as locals know it, is visible from the street by the 1950s themed signage and the lights and ruckus coming from within. The small space is visible in just a few windows, but this unassuming spot was Tallahassee's first brewery since Buckhead Brewing closed in 2003. Spend a few minutes in the place and the governing concept becomes abundantly clear—it's anything but boring.

When the owners of Fermentation Lounge decided to open a business, they originally wanted a movie theater that would serve craft beer and artisanal wine. The lounge adapted a 1950s theme from the logo to the furniture, and ran with it from there. The lounge is a place to sit, relax, and ferment, much like beer does in its tanks—The Ferm is like a brewing tank for people: a place for folks to lounge until they are finished fermenting. That concept evolved into a place where bar patrons in bathrobes randomly make ice cream with liquid nitrogen. Whether the Ferm is catering to the downtown business crowd from 4–7 p.m., or the twenty-five to thirty-five crowd until midnight, or college students after midnight, the lounge will be true to its guiding concept: anything is better than boredom.

This desire for entertainment carries over into the beer as well. Fermentation's brewer, Robert Clark, designs the beer to evoke an emotional response. Like so much else about Fermentation, the beer is designed to be memorable in one way or another. The beer is released sporadically in batches that make small brewers look huge: about ten or twenty gallons of beer at a time. At first, this much beer would last for weeks, then it would last for a week, and owing to the rise in popularity of both the lounge and craft beer, the releases last one evening and the beer is gone. The goal of the one-man brewing department is simply to make exceptional beer that showcases local ingredients. These ingredients could be anything from local honey, blueberries, watermelons, squash, pumpkins, persimmons, corn grits, or peaches to name a few past brewing ingredients. The beer is then brewed and fermented behind the bar in either a 14.5-gallon or a 27-gallon fermenter and served on an advertised night, when the beer is ready.

Fermentation Lounge is a unique experience in the craft beer world, and the beer pairs well with the kind of experience that the Ferm provides. On any given night, there will be a cast of characters that the best fiction writer could not come up with. Whether you are passing through for a beer or you are an insomniac, Fermentation will have a comfortable seat and a cold beer.

Insider Tip: Fermentation Lounge has recently stopped posting tappings of house beer on social media because there is so little of it. The only way to know if any house beers are on for sure is to call or stop by.

Proof Brewing Company

Brewery
1717 West Tennessee St., Tallahassee 32304
(850) 894-5638
http://www.proofbrewingco.com
Open 7 days a week

Proof began as a mild-mannered liquor store in 2008, then progressed into a bar, and in July of 2012, the metamorphosis was complete: Proof became Proof Brewing Company and offered its recipes for craft beer to Tallahassee. It became the capital city's largest craft brewery, currently producing about 500 barrels of beer yearly. Proof Brewing's bar doubles as the tasting room, both upstairs and down, and what looks like a trendy bar and package store functions as a proving ground for Proof's ales.

Proof is the natural product of a liquor store and bar staff growing increasingly curious about the products they sell. As Proof grew in knowledge, owner Byron Burroughs did both market research and product testing with the beers. At that point in time, summer of 2010, no one in Tallahassee was producing large-scale craft beer, so Byron continued to do his homework. Next, Proof Brewing bought fermenters and a three-barrel brewing system. As the research continued, the product testing began and Proof was licensed to serve beer on its premises and sell growlers to go. Slowly, other breweries came online, but none was the size and scope of what Proof wanted to be. When the time was right, and the recipes were tweaked and perfected to the staff's satisfaction, Proof started brewing commercially and sending kegs into distribution.

Proof Brewing serves up both an appreciation for the subtle nuances of sessionable beers and a respect for the intensity of bigger beers in the craft brew spectrum. While the brewery experiments with treating beers, barrel-aging beers, and rotating seasonals, there are five core brands that are the stalwarts of their lineup: a hop forward and big malt backbone american pale ale; a malty, spicy, citrusy rye ale; a bigger-than-pale-ale IPA, that makes the pale ale look like its little brother; an aggressive, floral, citrusy, and thick double IPA; and finally a roasty, chocolaty, and earthy stout.

The year 2013 will be big for Proof, as they signed a contract to move into a new twenty-barrel brewing system at the Railroad Square Art Park. This new facility will house 10,000 square feet of space, including brewery, biergarten, and lawn. Initially Proof will start out with 5,000 barrels of fermentation space, quickly advancing to 15,000 barrels when the time is right. The new facility will also house a canning line, and Proof will be packaging its beer in kegs, cans, and limited twenty-two-ounce bottles.

Insider Tip: Proof still operates Liquor Loft, one of the most highly regarded beer stores in Florida. Proof can offer one-of-a-kind house beers and beers from around the world for sale at the same address.

BREWERIES IN FERMENTATION

GrassLands Brewing Company

GrassLands Brewing Company began, like most breweries do, with love. Brewer Gabe Grass has a love for nature. Combined with his love for beer, the two ferment to form a brewery that promotes recycling, responsibility, and conservation in an industry that utilizes many resources to produce a final product. Grasslands' motto is Earth First Ales, a motto that stands for active involvement in conservation charities as well as use of organic ingredients wherever possible and a keen eye for recycling.

GrassLands Brewing knows of one ale it is considering as a core beer: Panhandle Amber Rye Ale. This beer blends the complexity of a rye ale with the maltiness of an amber ale and finds a nice balance between the two styles. Look for GrassLands to continue festival pours and progress toward a production brewery.

Canopy Roads Brewing Company

Canopy Roads Brewing Company has recently begun pouring at festivals and is working toward another production brewery in the Tallahassee area.

Ebb and Flow of Local Beer

Brewing in South Florida

SOUTH FLORIDA'S BREWING PAST

Miami's brewing history is as stable as the weather during hurricane season—breweries seem to wash in and out with the tide. As a tempest would break a levee, so Miami looks to be the breakers that washed out many an aspiring brewer. While many creative brewers bottled the breezes in the Magic City, not until the twenty-first century would South Florida boast breweries with staying power.

The ebb and flow of local beer in Miami follows most of the trends of Florida breweries save one: no brewery has withstood the undertow of the twentieth century. The rough waters began in 1913 when Dade County voted by a majority election to become a dry county. This would spell disaster for all of the county saloons that relied on alcohol sales to make their rent. It is surprising to think that anyone who lived in turn-of-the-century Miami did not consume alcohol on a regular basis considering the close proximity to the Everglades, mosquito swarms, sweltering heat, and monsoon-like rains. If there were any breweries extant during this time period before Prohibition, their names and faces have been lost in the tide as the county went dry, and the entire nation followed suit.

Prohibition Hits

Prohibition itself went fine in Miami, but Key West was another story. Local legend holds that Key West never officially recognized Prohibition, since the town's laid-back nature and distance from the mainland made regular contact virtually impossible and enforcement very difficult, considering that other Florida cities, like Tampa, were more populous, more metropolitan, and equally as "wet." Key West also proved to be a haven for rumrunners and smugglers of illicit goods from Cuba and the Bahamas, as noted in Hemingway's *To Have and Have Not*. Eventually, Key West was another affront to the crumbling wall of Prohibition.

After Prohibition: The Time of Many

Enter the 1930s: a time when America rediscovered alcoholic beverages of all sorts; even President Roosevelt declared, "it's time for a beer." Before Prohibition could be repealed, the Eighteenth Amendment was altered to allow for beer of 3.2 percent alcohol by volume. Beer was the only drink that could realistically fit this description, so beer was the first drink to return to the waiting glasses of parched patrons from sea to shining sea. Dozens of enterprising individuals across Florida sought to capitalize on the people's thirst. In 1933, the first brewery to open South Florida's beer floodgates was the Flamingo Brewing Company.

Flamingo Brewing was chartered as the Miami Brewing Company (as most breweries start off being named for their geographic region) but was soon altered to show its aspirations. Flamingo Brewing began building in December of 1933 and by July of 1934 had its first beers on the market. The brewery and bottling works was located at the corner of 22nd Street and 12th Avenue NW in Miami. The owners, George and Ernest Diehl, were probably associated with the Diehl Brewing family of Defiance, Ohio, who operated breweries both before and after Prohibition. The brewer was Robert Loewanthan, who received his brewing education in Chicago and his brewing experience at the Springfield Brewery of Ohio. All of the stones seemed to be falling into place to build a wall against the sea of changes swirling around Miami. Unfortunately, that sea would become Scylla and Charybdis and swallow the Flamingo. In January of 1935, approximately one year after opening, Flamingo Brewing announced that operations would cease and the brewing equipment would be listed for sale.

Around the time that Flamingo was opening, two other breweries were also forming: Hialeah Brewing Company in the Hialeah area of Miami and Sunshine Brewery of West Palm Beach. Both breweries would soon bend to the winds of change.

An industrial magnate and a banking investor in the Hialeah area of Miami founded Hialeah Brewing Company in 1934. The brewery was built at 699 Palm Avenue, at the corner of Palm Avenue and 6th Street. The brewery bottled Jockey Club Beer and Jockey Club Ale during most of 1934. Then it was closed and sold to another investor, who rechristened the facility The Miami Brewing Company. After the rebranding of the brewery and the restructuring of ownership, Miami Brewing Company began to make beer under the same brands as Hialeah Brewing. By the time 1935 rolled around, Miami Brewing was in the same financial trouble as its predecessor, and the brewery was sold again. By August of 1936, a new investor came in to buy the brewery, and like a phoenix, the Gold Top Brewing Company was reborn.

Miami also was home to the Wagner Brewery, located at 637 Northwest 13th Street. Wagner would be the longest running of Miami's Breweries, and like the others, began during this time period.

Miami's most infamous historical brewery opened in 1938 at the intersection of Northwest Seventh Avenue and Thirteenth Street

Lucky 7 Ale poster from Gold Top Brewing. Courtesy of Michael Zane.

as the Regal Brewery. In the tumult of 1939 Regal would sell to American Brewing of New Orleans and begin to produce one of Miami's most notorious beers: Regal Beer, in addition to Regal Ale and Great Dane Ale. As a brand, Regal would have staying power, but few who drank it wanted to remember the taste. Ironically, American Brewing and Regal Beer would become Miami's most enduring brewing operation.

Farther north in West Palm Beach, a new brewery was coming together. In 1934, the eye of the storm was churning out the Sunshine Brewery at 414 2nd Street. A local businessman, John T. Havens, opened the brewery on the site of a former laundry, and brewed Havens Sunshine Ale, Havens Pilsner, and All American Lager in bottles and kegs for the Miami area. The brewery's slogans bragged to customers that the beer was "Not a Burp in a Barrel," and the beer itself was "Completely Digestible." The brewer was a sixty-year-old German man, and the beer sold for five cents a glass. Prosperity would not last for the burpless beers, for in 1936 the brewery was bought out by the then-manager of the Wagner Brewing Company of Miami, William Gould. Gould reshaped his brewery in his image and likeness: where once trod Sunshine Brewery now went the Gould Brewing Company. After modernizing and doubling brewing capacity, Gould Brewing began brewing Gould's All-Grain

Beer (made of malt, hops, and rice) and Gould's Old English Type Ale.

Like a novel trying to limp without its title character, the Gould Brewing Company could not go on without William Gould, who left the brewery for an opening in sales at the Jax Brewing Company of Jacksonville. Mr. Gould must have read the writing on the wall because Jax Brewery would last several decades longer than the sinking ship of a brewery he ran, and Gould Brewing would be reborn one final time—in this new life it was renamed Tuna Brewing Company. Tuna Brewing would advertise to the brewing community a production of 10,000 barrels of beer in 1939. While the labels of Tuna's beers were wildly colorful, apparently the business plan was not since Tuna Brewing did not last an entire year except as a doomed paper corporation. Even the paper corporation of Tuna Brewing did not take long to get canned by the government because the owners failed to pay their taxes.

All of the breweries in Florida, except the soon-to-be extinct Tuna Brewery banded together in April of 1934 to form the Florida Brewers' Alliance.

The year 1939 was like a whirlwind, as breweries all over Miami were adjusting to the doldrums of business and hoping for an oncoming boom. That boom would come in the form of World War II spending, and the breweries that lasted into the 1940s would enjoy the same bustling business that other breweries in Florida would bask in.

After the Many: The Time of Regal

The only brewery in Miami to weather the tempests that came after World War II was Regal Brewery, and it did so by promoting the beer locally. One of Regal's slogans after World War II, recalled by a former Regal truck driver: "You can't drink freight." Regal was appealing to the locals and tourists who wanted fresh beer but could not afford anything else. While it was true that Regal was more affordable because there were no freight costs to deliver it to local markets, the brand's reputation was quickly reduced to a "cheap beer"; in the 1950s ninety-nine cents could buy three quarts of Regal beer.

Regal continued after the 1950s; then in 1958, Anheuser-Busch marched into Miami with the intent to buy Regal. This was around the same time that Anheuser was making other investments and buying other properties across the Sunshine State, and so the federal government was keeping an eye on it. In 1961, an antitrust suit forced Anheuser-Busch to divest itself of National Brewery, and Regal Beer continued into the 1960s, when a Baltimore firm invested a reported three million dollars in Regal. Regal continued to stumble along as a beer preferred for its inexpensive quantity with no comment toward its quality. Regal was almost completely removed from the minds of the people of Miami. In 1973, the *Miami Herald* published an article entitled "Yes, Folks, There Is a Miami Beer." That headline would prove to be an ironic death knell for the long-standing brewery, which closed shortly afterward.

After Regal unto the Millennium

After Regal folded in the 1970s, many breweries would come and go in the Miami area. Some of the beers of this era still survive, but in recipe only, when the Florida Beer Company brews them.

The 1990s showed a resurgence of fresh local beer, but the population was not ready to support such businesses. The Florida Beer Company of Melbourne now brews Miami Brewing's Hurricane Reef beers, but there is discussion of retiring these brands. The Key West Brewing Company, the Old Florida Brewing Company, along with the Hops chain of brewpubs, and the Prince-Wiest Brewing Company all have had grand closings around Miami. Hammerhead's Brewpub opened and closed on Duval Street in Key West. Several breweries even report exceptional production numbers: the Killian-Bayer Brewing Company of Fort Meade claimed 50,000 barrels of beer in the late '90s, in a time when other breweries state-wide were struggling to produce 1,000 barrels, and the Ybor City Brewing Company was claiming 15,000 barrels. These numbers are essentially unsubstantiated, as the breweries are defunct and the records to support them may be lost to history.

Two Miami breweries were around long enough to make some splashes in the *Miami Herald*: Firehouse Brewing and Miami Brewing Company. In an article written about the up-and-coming Brautech Brewing Company, which set up a twenty-five-barrel brewing system in 1996, the *Miami Herald* comments on the current state of craft beer competition in Miami-Dade.

Brautech Brewing was setting up to make a run at brewing 10,000 barrels of beer in 1996. It planned to be in Miami bars and on Miami shelves by September 1996. Apparently Brautech had family members who were in the beer business from Guyana and Nicaragua, and ten people on staff before beginning production. That is especially ambitious in light of how some of Florida's current largest craft breweries began operations: Cigar City Brewing began with two people on staff.

Firehouse Brewing owner Christopher Schalk spoke of South Florida being "virgin territory," and he dreamt of expanding into the Caribbean, Central, and South America. "Why beat each other up in North America when there's so much growth potential in Miami and to the south?" The echoes of irony resound through history with that comment; as of 2014 Florida supports more than one hundred breweries and brewpubs. Schalk talked about his projections for Firehouse's annual production, and put his brewery somewhere around the 4,000–6,000-barrel mark. Firehouse Brewing was located at 7902 Northwest 64th Street in Miami, and according to the web closed its doors in 1998.

By far the most interesting comment on Miami beer came from Miami Brewing Company founder Rick Durkin. Durkin's company, located at 9292 101st Street in Miami, was planning on producing 7,500 barrels of beer in 1996. All of these beers, unbeknownst to Durkin, would have their recipes turned over to Florida Beer Company within ten years. Durkin was quoted in the South Florida Business Journal as saying, "The biggest problem that all the microbreweries will have is in actually getting on the shelves at supermarkets . . . we have no expectation that all our beers will get on the shelves at Publix's smaller stores." Durkin stated that Miami had ample room for the growth of local microbreweries, but he predicted a "fierce battle for shelf space."

As the door closed on Miami's breweries of the nineties, a new door opened at the beginning of the millennium for breweries like Kelly's Caribbean Grille and Brewery, which had the backing of '80s icon Kelly McGillis and her husband in Key West. Miami would then get a new brewery and winery in Schnebly Redlands, but the brewery would not come until 2012.

Many brewers came to South Florida with dreams of sunsets and drafts of ales, but none of those breweries lasted into the twenty-first century. It would not be until after the new millennium that the new wave of South Florida Breweries would come in and leave a lasting mark on the Magic City, the Conch Republic, the City of Palms, and beyond.

Breweries like Wynwood Brewing, Gravity Brewlab, and J. Wakefield Brewery had literally to work for years to open breweries in Miami-Dade. While Gravity is still working toward opening, Wynwood Brewing opened in late 2013, and J. Wakefield in early 2014—all of them having endured a long road to the first pour.

Titanic Brewery Company

Brewpub
5813 Ponce de Leon Blvd., Coral Gables 33416
(305) 668-1742
http://titanicbrewery.com
Open 7 days a week

Titanic Brewery got its name from Miami's status as the cruise capital of the world. This nautical-themed brewpub is situated just north of the University of Miami campus in Coral Gables. With front windows onto Ponce de Leon Boulevard, Titanic serves up brewpub fare with a clear glass window to the brewery and the line of tanks behind the bar. The beer does not go very far in the lines, as Titanic moves the beer from fermentation into serving tanks and right from the brewery to the bar. The beer served is the beer

brewed not thirty feet from where patrons sit. The beer is very fresh when it's served, and they use a small system to cycle through the beers and ensure fresh beer is always on hand. The cozy pub serves English, German, and American-style beers regularly to accompany the different tastes of the surrounding area.

Brewer Scott Copeland is a veteran Miami brewer, having experienced brewing life at Miami's defunct Firehouse Brewery; he now brings his years of experience to Titanic. Titanic's core brands of Triple Screw German Pilsner, Captain Smith Rye Ale, White Star IPA, Britannic Best Bitter, Boiler Room Nut Brown Ale, and Ship Builder Oatmeal Stout are always on hand. With these beers, Titanic tries to run the spectrum of light to dark beers—starting with a light German pilsner and gradually getting darker and heavier until reaching an oatmeal stout, which is heavy enough for a stout fan, yet light for a stout at 6 percent ABV. Titanic also spices up its lineup with seasonals rotating in and out that may include a Belgian blonde, a German dunkel, or a citrus hop bomb of a double IPA.

Friendly, open, and warm, Titanic is the kind of neighborhood pub where anyone would feel comfortable. Its beers represent a diverse collection of styles, and its pub fare ensures that there is an opportunity to enjoy the entire repertoire. Titanic varies its beers, serves in pints and stemware, and rotates guest taps to provide an extended variety of choices.

The Abbey Brewing Company

Contract Brewery
1115 16th Street, Miami Beach 33139
(305) 538-8110
http://abbeybrewinginc.com
Open 7 days a week

Upon walking into the Abbey, this all-wood bar and its cozy surroundings give the feeling of a fire-lit English pub or a Belgian abbey. With a well-stocked tap list, including beers whose recipes originated with the owner (they are contract brewed in Melbourne), the Abbey is the kind of place that is great to visit any time life requires reflection and a beer, or just a beer.

The owner and head brewer, Raymond Ragazio, opened the Abbey in 1995 in South Beach, Miami. This area was not a place that craft beer lovers sought out, but tourists certainly did, and the Abbey established itself as a place that made beer and made a great tap list out of the beers available in Florida. The Abbey has lasted longer than any other brewery in Miami history and continues going strong.

The Abbey has four core beers Ragazio designed for the bar. All of the Abbey's beers are designed to be contemplated, as they all have layers of flavor, but be warned, the beers also have a fair amount of alcohol bite. The Abbey serves a 6.2 percent ABV citrus-hoppy Immaculate IPA, a 9.5 percent coffee and licorice-laced Father Theodore's Stout, a 10 percent raisiny and fruity Brother Dan's Double, and a 12 percent toffee and candy sugar forward Brother Aaron's Quadruple. The Abbey works to keep all of four of these beers on draft and maintains the other ten taps with craft beer from around Florida and around the country. The Abbey keeps national and Florida breweries on tap as well, but the Abbey's beer, which is made at the Florida Beer Company, keeps up with the national brands.

The Abbey makes what would normally be merely a beach stop into a beer stop. The Abbey's four core beers are worth considering on a stop at this Miami Beach landmark, a craft beer stop before there were any others on Miami Beach.

Insider Tip: Parking in Miami Beach can get a bit precarious. Don't be afraid to park where a space presents itself and walk a bit to the Abbey. The work is worth it.

Big Bear Brewing Company

Brewpub
1800 North University Drive, Coral Springs 33071
(954) 341-5545
http://www.bigbearbrewingco.com
Open 7 days a week

Big Bear Brewing Company has the look and feel of an upscale brewpub with beers that can be appreciated by any type of beer lover. The restaurant offers great food to pair with the beers, and like any great brewpub, Big Bear works its beer into the food.

Big Bear Brewing Company set down roots and opened its doors in 1997, at the same time that many of the state's first small brewers began brewing since the mass local brewery extinction of the

1960s. Its restaurant concept revolves around creating sauces, soups, desserts, and entrees, which are prepared fresh daily, in a manner that incorporates the beer into the food. Much of Big Bear's staff has been with it since the beginning of the pub, and head brewer Matt Cox oversees all of Big Bear's unique offerings—some of the first and finest craft beer in South Florida.

Big Bear Brewing covers the gamut of beer styles and rotates several taps regularly to continuously offer something new, interesting, and seasonal. Big Bear's roasty chocolaty Black Bear Stout hugs the stout lover while a rotating berry beer tap is there to encourage those who are just discovering fresh craft beers. Big Bear's year-round offerings include Polar Light, a light 4.9 percent American ale; Hibernation pale ale, a hoppy 6.5 percent pale ale hopped with Cascade hops; Grizzly red ale, an Irish-style red ale that combines the maltiness of an Irish red with some of the hop profile of an American amber; Brown Bear brown ale, a 6 percent medium-bodied brown ale with some dark flavors and bitterness; and Kodiak Belgian dubbel, a sweet banana-and-clove forward ale made in the style of a Belgian specialty beer. Seasonal and rotating taps can yield anything from a hop-forward IPA to a light raspberry ale to the roasty, chocolaty Black Bear stout.

Big Bear's convenient location to both Alligator Alley and I-95 make it an ideal stop in the Coral Springs area. Its draw of fresh, innovative beers and fresh ingredients make any meal a great pairing with a pouring from the tap.

The Funky Buddha Lounge and Brewery

Brewery
2621 North Federal Highway, Boca Raton 33431
(561) 368-4643
http://www.thefunkybuddha.com
Open 7 days a week

The Funky Buddha Lounge and Brewery is the beer equivalent to the crazy cousin that just won't sit still. The owner and brewer work together to create some of the most outstanding and flavorful beers—the kind of beer that must be sampled to be believed. From a Peanut Butter and Jelly beer to a Maple Bacon Coffee Porter to a Starfruit Berliner Weiss to a Peanut Butter Cup Stout, the Funky Buddha keeps cranking out the hits in a fun, upbeat environment that hosts beer enthusiasts and concertgoers alike.

When the Funky Buddha began in September of 2010, it was a small lounge and brewery near the beach in Boca Raton. The origi-

nal brewer, Kevin Abbot, comes from a wine background. He is a former sommelier who left the wine industry for the deeper flavors and broader diversity of beer. Funky Buddha Brewery began as a project to brew beer and teach other interested friends to brew. The Buddha began with a tiny thirty-five-gallon brewing system and gained national attention while brewing on one of the smallest systems in the state. After the United States began to turn its eyes toward Funky Buddha, the owners decided to find a new home and brew their beers on a larger scale, with a dream of making them available to the entire state of Florida.

Funky Buddha has several core beers on tap at all times. The core lineup begins with hefeweizen that yields banana and fruity notes in a German wheat beer. Next on draft rises a malty red ale dubbed Red Dawn. Buzzing the tower after Red Dawn is a citrusy IPA with the moniker Hop Gun, followed by the dark and sultry sweet OP Porter. The Buddha also puts on numerous different, weird, off-kilter, and one-of-a-kind beers on any given night. Opening the door on any night of the week could yield a taste of a twisted beer like the purple-hued Blueberry Tart Ale, No Crusts Peanut Butter and Jelly Brown Ale, Starfruit Berliner Weisse, a tart Florida Weisse with tangy starfruit added, or Last Snow, a porter that erupts with flavors of coconut and chocolate with every sip. With a thirty-five-gallon brewing system at the lounge, Funky Buddha can turn over plenty of beer in a short span of time.

Funky Buddha has made its reputation with solid core beers and consistent yet interesting left-field type beers. Funky Buddha began distribution of its beer around South Florida but has not lost touch with its roots—the owners bought a new and larger pilot system for Oakland Park, so the funky beers will continue to flow.

Insider Tip: The Funky Buddha Lounge and Brewery is open very late. Beer travelers can combine its late hours with many hotels nearby, making the Lounge an ideal last stop on any beer tour.

Funky Buddha Brewery

Brewery
1201 NE 38th Street, Oakland Park 33334
(954) 440-0046
http://www.funkybuddhabrewery.com
Open 7 days a week

The Funky Buddha Lounge and Brewery began with a mission to provide fresh, bold, and innovative craft beer to the South Florida area, and while the beers certainly won the brewery widespread acclaim, the original thirty-five-gallon brewing system would not be enough to spread beer nirvana around Florida. So, in summer of 2013, the Funky Buddha owners, Ryan and KC Sentz, cut the ribbon on the newest Funky Buddha temple: the Funky Buddha Production Brewery in Oakland Park.

The opening of the new facility gave Funky Buddha breathing room while allowing it to send more than a few kegs into distribution. The only problem has been keeping up with the demand. If demand for beer from the old location was intense, demand for beer from the Oakland Park location has only increased. The new Oakland Park location boasts a thirty-barrel commercial brewing system and the ability to keg beer beyond the lounge's wildest dreams. The brewing and kegging abilities alongside a three-barrel pilot system allow the new Funky Buddha to stay true to the old Funky Buddha's spirit of innovation and envelope-pushing beers that astound even the harshest beer critics. The new brewery will allow the Sentz brothers to produce their core beers on a scale thirty times larger than before, but the pilot system will allow the brewery to continue brewing small batches of the beer that made it famous, like Maple Bacon Coffee Porter, a beer whose taste profile lives up to the name without the addition of any pork products; Bonita Applebaum, an apple pie ale that tastes like it just came out of the oven; and Sweet

Potato Casserole, a beer that tastes like it should come with marsh-mallow glaze over the glass.

Funky Buddha's beers are currently distributed in the South Florida Market.

Tequesta Brewing Company

Brewery
287 South US Highway 1, Tequesta 33469
(561) 745-5000
https://tequestabrewing.com
Closed Monday

This small yet fierce brewery in the tiny beach town of Tequesta has grown immensely to become one of Florida's premiere East Coast breweries. Tequesta Brewing Company endeavors to make its beers a little bit of everything—clean beers brewed to style and to a high standard of quality.

Brewer and manager Matt Webster began home brewing seventeen years before opening Tequesta Brewing Company, includ-

ing making small batches of beer for the neighboring café, then known as Corner Café and Brewery. Corner Café's brewery became so popular that the space next door was procured and the tasting room has taken over as Tequesta Brewery's showpiece. The original 1915 bar in Tequesta's tasting room came from a friend who saved it from a bar his grandfather ran nightly after his day job as a coal miner had ended. The bar was shipped to Tequesta with the original glass intact and installed in the brewery tasting room. The impressive wooden bar is a doff of the cap to the line of proud brewers and their line of work dating back to before Prohibition. The bar is one in a line of details that Tequesta Brewing pays careful attention to as it pours out liquid labor for its patrons.

Tequesta is currently using a fifteen-barrel brewery and is working to its fullest capacity to produce the best beer it can make. The brewery opened in 2011 and produced 1,500 barrels of beer in its first year. The brewers hope to increase production and continue until they can outgrow their current space. Upon maxing out, they hope to open another facility in Palm Beach Gardens or nearby to keep thirsty South Florida hydrated. Tequesta Brewing is working to keep its consumers educated about beer since Florida was a bit behind in the craft brewing revolution. Tequesta is currently distributed from Jacksonville all the way to the southernmost point in the United States; the next step will begin as soon as it is feasible: canning the beers. The brewery hopes to grow as organically as possible, to 4,000–5,000 barrels of production in the near future.

Tequesta Brewing is a small pub a few blocks from the beach in a quiet area of Florida's east coast. If its Belgian Saison or Chancellor Kolsh is any indication, it will not be quiet for much longer. As Tequesta grows, so shall demand for their beach-perfect beers, summer afternoon ales, and big-hitting bruisers.

Insider Tip: Corner Café is still open next door to the brewery and will serve a great breakfast alongside one of Tequesta's beers.

Tampa Bay Brewing Company Coral Springs Tap House

Brewery
1221 North University Drive, Coral Springs 33307
(954) 227-2337
http://coralspringstaphouse.com
Open 7 days a week

The Tampa Bay Brewing Company Coral Springs Tap House is home to a second brewery for the Doble family, who owns the original Tampa Bay Brewing Company in Ybor City. The Coral Springs tap house receives shipments of Tampa Bay Brewing Company beers from the pub in Ybor City, but head brewer Dave Doble and a few intrepid brewers keep most of the beer at the TBBC Coral Springs tap room stocked from the TBBC brewing equipment in Coral Springs.

TBBC Coral Springs is known to keep the standard Old Elephant Foot IPA and One Night Stand Pale Ale along with some Jack the Quaffer Porter, but the Coral Springs tap room makes some differences between them and the mother ship: expect new and different beers when in Coral Springs. Beers like the light and refreshing Rice Rice Baby Rice Pale Ale, the 6.2 percent ABV No Daves Pale Ale (no one named Dave was involved in the brewing of this beer), Wooly Mammoth IPA, an IPA that delivers a hop punch like its namesake, and the malty Kennedy Scotch Ale Select grace only the taps of TBBC Coral Springs.

What is the main difference between Tampa Bay Brewing in Ybor City and Tampa Bay Brewing in Coral Springs? The Tampa Bay Brewing Company in Ybor City is an award-winning pub that incorporates beer into many dishes. The Tampa Bay Brewing Company in Coral Springs is a brewery that adds to the reputation of the Ybor pub but does not serve an ounce of food.

Schnebly Redland's Winery and Brewery (Miami Brewing)

Brewery
30205 Southwest 217th Ave., Homestead 33030
(305) 242-1224
http://www.schneblywinery.com/
Open 7 days a week

Schnebly's is Florida's southernmost combination winery and brewery, having the ambiance of a California winery with the tropical fruit infusions of Florida's climate. While the brewery is in its infancy, the winery has been making tropical fruit-centric wines for several years. The owners decided to build a biergarten on the grounds of the winery, and they began the journey toward becoming Homestead's combination winery and brewery.

Schnebly Redland's Winery and Brewery is the brainchild of owner Peter Schnebly and brewer Mauricio Mejia. The Schnebly

family began as a produce company and then focused on wines, ultimately progressing until a brewery was brought to being in 2011. The brewery currently occupies a space that was once a storage facility for produce, with many of the brewing tanks being manufactured by winery staff after delays in manufacture and steep costs in shipping hurt the brewery.

The Schnebly Brewery has four core beers that are on at all times. Big Rod is a blonde ale with notes of coconut mixed with light malts and some nuances of tropical fruit. Gator Tail Brown Ale is a brown ale with notes of roasted nuts, chocolate, and coffee. Shark Attack Wheat Ale is a sessionable wheat beer at 5.3 percent alcohol and has light hints of bread and citrus. Finally, Speed Way IPA has an English quality to it with mild hops and some grassy flavors mixed in amongst some of the caramel character.

Homestead is known for its agricultural stylings and the cornucopia of tropical fruit it produces. Schnebly Redland's harnesses the well of tropical fruit, the bountiful Florida sunshine, and the breezy South Florida flavors to produce its beers.

Insider Tip: Schnebly's brewery operates out of the winery on some of the most unique grounds in Florida. Its setup makes an ideal spot for a beer-against-wine pairing matchup.

J. Wakefield Brewing Company

Brewery
120 Northwest 24th Street, Miami 33127
http://www.jwakefieldbrewing.com

J. Wakefield Brewing Company began in brewer Johnathan Wakefield's garage as a hobby. One thing led to another and Wakefield has been making waves across Florida since 2010, when his beers were brewed at Cigar City and poured at its annual Hunahpu Day festivities. Wakefield's meteoric rise among craft beer enthusiasts has been swift, and with the addition of JWB's production brewery, look for Wakefield Brewing's uber-hazy, pink or purple tinted Florida weisses across South Florida.

Wakefield announced in 2013 that he has secured a fifteen-barrel production brewing system and opened his commercial brewery in the Wynwood district of Miami in 2014. The brewery allows Wakefield a home base to start from so his supporters can enjoy his beer, and Wakefield has more fans than some Florida sports teams. In 2013, when Wakefield launched his fundraising campaign on Crowdbrewed.com, he hoped to raise $55,000 in a month and a half to fund his brewery. Wakefield reached his goal in twenty-six hours. While the campaign remained open, Wakefield was able to raise over $106,000 in less than one month. As Wakefield was eager to get JWB off the ground, so too was the community of Florida beer lovers.

Wakefield will anchor his brewery with four flagship beers: the sessionable hop bomb called Hops in Session; the banana-forward hefeweizen known as El Jefe; a brown ale brewed with Yerba Mate called Mate Bliss; and in a nod to vintage video games and roasty beers all at once, a porter dubbed Master Blaster Porter. Wakefield has promised Florida that he will devote 75 percent of his brewery's resources to his core and seasonal beers, and the rest of his efforts will be devoted to his Florida weisses, which will display the wide array of tropical fruit grown in the Miami area such as guava, passion fruit, mango, and guanabana.

Wakefield himself is easy enough to spot; he's usually the tallest man in the room at over six feet, two inches. He also pours the colorful beers out of tap handles that reference comic books like *Thor* and television shows of yesteryear like *The Thundercats*. J. Wakefield Brewing's beers are available in the South Florida market.

Insider Tip: Wakefield has made quite a name for himself collaborating with Florida brewers. Watch for sporadic return collaborations.

Wynwood Brewing Company

Brewery
565 Northwest 24th Street, Miami 33127
(305) 982-8732
http://www.wynwoodbrewing.com
Closed Monday

Wynwood Brewing Company is the vision of Luis Brignoni made real by his blistering work and tireless effort. Wynwood Brewing is opening in Miami's Wynwood district and will be the first production brewery to open in Miami proper since the Wagner Brewing Company did so after Prohibition. The brewery has suffered several setbacks including the death of former brewmaster Jim Patton, founder of the national Abita Brewery of Louisiana, who signed on to be Wynwood's founding brewer. Jim's death was a painful blow to the team at Wynwood, but Brignoni promised to push on in Jim's memory. After a search, he recruited brewer Nik Mebane who got his brewing education at Otto's Pub in State College, Pennsylvania, and moved to South Florida to work for the Miami Gordon Biersch restaurant. When Biersch closed the Miami location, Mebane signed on with Wynwood to help spearhead Wynwood's brewing efforts. Nik is looking forward to helping build a genuine craft beer culture in the Magic City. In addition to Nik and Luis Brignoni Jr. and Sr., Wynwood's cellarman is David Rodriguez, one of the founding members of Brew F.I.U., a culture of home brewers centered on Florida International University.

Wynwood Brewing Company elected to use a fifteen-barrel brewhouse to produce its beers. As a new brewery on Miami's block, Wynwood Brewing has announced several core beers and two seasonal/rotating beers. Wynwood's anchor beers start with the bready and sweet 5 percent ABV La Rubia Blonde Ale. Next in line stands Wynwood IPA, a 7.2 percent ABV India Pale Ale dry-hopped for flavors of aromatic citrus. The final mainstay of Wynwood's lineup is Pop's Porter, weighing in at 6.2 percent alcohol and bringing flavors of roasted malts, chocolate, and coffee. Wynwood also plans to rotate seasonal beers like Lupulado, a fresh hop IPA where different varieties of hops can be used to show off different flavors; NagaSake, a pale ale aged on sake-soaked oak chips and The Stiglitz, an Oktoberfest hopped with a tropical fruit hop.

The Wynwood team is very proud of the area it chose for the brewery. The tap handles are modeled after a spray can since spray can art is synonymous with the Wynwood Arts District and displays the pride the team feels in its neighborhood. Look for Wynwood beers on draft and eventually in bottles in South Florida.

Brewzzi (Boca Raton and West Palm Beach)

Brewpub
2222 Glades Road, Boca Raton 33431
(561) 392-BREW
http://www.brewzzi.com/
700 South Rosemary Ave., West Palm Beach 33401
(561) 366-9785
Open 7 days a week

Brewzzi is an upscale pub with a brewery in the back through a glass partition; or a brewery with a restaurant visible through a fishbowl, depending on perspective. The pub serves up a rotating menu of old world Italian and Americana while the brewery matches the food with a palette of lagers and ales.

Brewzzi opened in 1997 during a time when craft beer was just beginning to surge up from the depths to which it had been banished when larger production breweries moved into Florida. The Boca Raton pub used to be an old bank, and all of the old facilities were converted when the brewery bought the building. The brewery still operates in the space that was the bank's vault. The vault

was opened up and separated with a glass wall and now diners can see the beer they drink being made feet from their tables. The pub has two locations, and the beers in Boca Raton are brewed by head brewer Matt Manthe who came to Brewzzi after studying at the renowned Siebel Institute and touring Germany to study brewing science. Brewzzi's West Palm Beach location is anchored by Reinhard Knieriemen, who also favors and respects German beers and makes a mean German Alt. While the two locations maintain different rotating beers, they offer the same core beers in each restaurant: the light and lagered Boca Blonde, weighing in at 4.5 percent alcohol; the CityFest Vienna Lager at 4 percent alcohol; Black Duke, a German Shwarzbier containing some cocoa notes and a light body, also showing 4 percent alcohol. While these seem like the lightest beers because of their alcohol content, Brewzzi packs a doozy of flavor into each one, and the alcohol content allows for multiple beers and conversation before the night is over. Continue to look for special beers flowing out of Brewzzi's fishbowl brewery from time to time; those experimental beers could be an IPA with Jade hops raising a taste of pineapple, passionfruit, and grapefruit, it could be a barrel-aged English Old Ale showing notes of vanilla, toffee, and oak, or it could be a Belgian Quadruple with flavors of candy sugar and plums, and that is not even mentioning Firkin Wednesday on the first Wednesday of every month.

Brewzzi is a brewpub in an area that appreciates lagers and their place in the scorching South Florida sun. Whether you're local to it or an out-of-town visitor, look for tasty German-style beers and Americana cuisine pairing with the periodic brewer's select tap handles. Brewzzi is a unique spoke in the revolution of the South Florida Craft Beer Wheel.

Kelly's Caribbean Bar, Grille, and Brewery

Brewpub
301 Whitehead Street, Key West 33040
(305) 293-8484
http://www.kellyskeywest.com/
Open 7 days a week

Only Kelly's Caribbean Bar, Grille, and Brewery holds the distinction of being America's southernmost brewery. Housed in the Conch Republic of Key West, Kelly's pours its beer while wild roosters roam the streets, and tourists in search of local beer come to sample the wares. Kelly's core beers are mainstays of the island and pair well with beachside fare, a Key West sunset, and the din of travelers meandering toward Mallory Square.

The story of Kelly's place starts long before the brewery and grill occupied the space. It begins on the site of a runway of Mechem

Field in Key West where the first international flight in the United States departed for Cuba. The building that now houses Kelly's was the headquarters for Pan American Airways, which began as a mail and passenger service between Key West and Cuba in 1927. Time came and went; businesses came and took over the building, and all folded. The brewery still displays some of the pictures and signs that show off its storied history. In 1991, the property that is now Kelly's was purchased by its permanent owner, actress Kelly McGillis, the star of the iconic *Top Gun* and *Witness*. McGillis converted the place into the restaurant and began the brewing process shortly after in 1992. It was in owning the bar that Kelly met her wife, Melanie Leis, who did a stint as a bartender for the restaurant. Leis and McGillis wed in a civil union ceremony in 2010.

The storied Kelly's keeps three beers on tap at all times: the light and mildly citrusy Southern Clipper Wheat Beer, the light and somewhat sweet Key West Golden Ale, and the malty Havana Red Ale. All of the beers pay tribute to the history of the brewery and the island it calls home. All of these ales ferment in about fourteen days on Kelly's seven-barrel brewing system, and all are brewed to German standards, meaning that there are no additives, no fruit, no spices, and no surprises in the beer. The only ingredients allowed under the Purity Law, or Reinheisgebot, are malted barley or wheat, water, yeast, and hops. Kelly's will also cycle through the occasional seasonal beer or brewer's choice tap, but like the sunrise after a storm, these three are certain to be pouring on any night in the Florida Keys.

Kelly's is a Key West brewpub that has survived time, tide, hurricane, wars, and tourists to become what it is today. As much as there is to say about Key West, it will be a herculean task to find another brewery in the United States that will serve tasty Caribbean food while roosters roam the street, drag queens dance their dances, and sea breezes blow away trouble. Kelly's is the only place that can currently pair those Key West staples with a house beer.

Naples Beach Brewery

Brewery
4110 Enterprise Ave., Suite 217, Naples 34104
(239) 304-8795
http://www.naplesbeachbrewery.com/
Open Friday and Saturday

While the outside bears a nondescript, warehouse façade, the inside of this southwest Florida brewery shows the determination of brewers to bring local craft beer to the thirsty Naples and Fort Myers community. Naples Beach Brewery stands with the distinction of being southwest Florida and Collier County's first local craft brewery, and although it is small, it is growing by leaps and bounds in an area that before 2012 never had a craft brewery of its own.

Naples Beach Brewery owner, Will Lawson, is a Michigan transplant to the sunny shores of Florida. Will was a golf course management major until family and a passion for beer moved him to South Florida's Naples Beach. He attended the Siebel Institute for Brewing; then he lined up a 1.5-barrel brewing system, some 3-barrel fermenters, and a space in an industrial park and began the journey that is now Naples Beach Brewery. Once zoning and licensing were complete, the brewery began pouring its beer in June of 2012. Will has worked to do a fair amount of consumer education—teaching the community, comprising both tourists and locals, about the advantages of fresh beer.

Naples Beach's beers seek an appeal to the everyday drinker and acknowledge the need for beer that is relatively low in alcohol while delivering lots of flavor, beers that are not assertive to the point of detracting from overall character. While Naples Beach is still developing its core beers, one of its mainstays will be a red ESB called Rojo Especial. Rojo clocks in at 5.2 percent alcohol by volume and has a big caramel and toffee malt presence with a mild fruitiness

toward the finish. This light-bodied and easy-drinking ESB will be Naples Beach Brewing's core, followed by a developing lineup and a rotation of seasonals like Weizen, Pale Ale, Black IPA, Mango Ginger Tripel, Imperial Pub Ale (IPA), and Stout.

Look for Naples Beach on draft throughout southwest Florida in pubs and fine establishments, including at the brewery tours and tastings that Will hosts most Fridays and Saturdays. Naples Beach also has plans to build a tasting room and expand its brewing ability when the time is right.

Due South Brewing Company

Brewery
2900 High Ridge Rd. #3, Boynton Beach 33426
(561) 463-2337
http://www.duesouthbrewing.com/
Closed Monday

Due South is a young brewery with big dreams and a quickly expanding reach. Its warehouse space in Boynton Beach (park in the back) also houses the tasting room, which looks out over the brewery. The laid-back environment syncs with South Florida's beaches and breezes, and when the warehouse is open and the dry wind blows through, it creates a perfect scene for craft beer.

Due South is owned by brewer Mike Halker, who began home brewing because his wife was allergic to the sulfites in wine. Once Mike began, he worked out the recipe for a beer that his wife would enjoy, and Due South's core beer dubbed Caramel Cream Ale was born. Mike won awards for his home brew, which encouraged him

to move to the next level and become a commercial brewer. Once he moved to Boynton Beach, he began the long journey that would culminate in opening a brewery. Mike had to work with the city to rewrite existing codes so that he could open a commercial brewery; then his landlord backed out, and he had to restart the brewery project. Luckily, after nine weeks of permitting, several thousand dollars, and much sweat, Due South opened in May of 2012 and began distributing shortly afterward. Since South Florida in general and Boynton specifically are known for snowbirds and tourists, as well as locals who aren't really familiar with craft beer, Due South has been doing a lot of talking about its beers and working its fifteen-barrel system to slake South Florida's locals and tourists alike.

Due South's warehouse brewery and tasting room is the epicenter of its beers. They brew the types of beers that the staff likes to drink, and luckily, they have good taste. With the sweet and light Caramel Cream Ale at the helm and the likes of hop-forward Category Three IPA anchoring the core lineup, the tasting room flows with Due South and other Florida breweries' beers. Aside from the core lineup, Due South also rotates seasonal and experimental beers. The spring of 2013 saw a hoppy pale ale made with Pacific area hops as well as a Café Ole Espresso Porter. The beers are only available due south in Florida—from Jupiter to Key West.

Look for Due South to become one of the big names in South Florida beer in the coming years as other craft breweries expand, too. Due South has added fermenters, and continues to do so, along with several racks of barrels for barrel aging. Due South has a 15,000-square-foot warehouse that it is working to grow in, and since more growth means more beer, Due South will grow as much as Boynton and its beaches will allow.

Insider Tip: Due South fills only growlers purchased from Due South.

Fort Myers Brewing Company

Brewery
12811 Commerce Lakes Drive, Suite 27–28, Fort Myers 33913
(239) 313-6576
http://www.facebook.com/FMBrew
Open Thursday through Sunday

Lee County's first craft brewery was the outgrowth of the craft beer movement in California. Fort Myers Brewing's head brewer, Rob Wyte, has worked with Oceanside Ale Works in California, and when he moved to Fort Myers he was astounded to see that there was no local craft brewery in his county. Like many enterprising brewers in the craft beer movement, Rob decided to make beer for his fellow man in the City of Palms, rather than just drink what was available.

Rob could not have picked a better spot—Fort Myers Brewing occupies space in an industrial park just minutes from the stadium where the Boston Red Sox have their spring training. The brewery

opened in March of 2013, and judging by the reception of opening day, Fort Myers is as excited to have a craft brewery as the brewery is to be pouring beers. The warm reception arrived while Fort Myers Brewing was pouring everything it could make in its seven-barrel system, and considering that Wyte had to have neck surgery the week before the brewery's opening. Friends and family helped Wyte with brewing and after that he toughed out as much as he could to prep the brewery to meet the new neighbors on opening day. Wyte estimates that the brewery had 1,200–1,500 people attend the first day of pouring. He comes to that conclusion because the line for a beer was forty-five minutes long, every parking space was full in the industrial park, and the local food truck ran out of food in three hours.

Most of Fort Myers's beer names come from local geography, with one exception that honors the brewery's past: Red Tap Red Ale. The malty and somewhat citrusy red ale honors the tenacity of the brewery and its patrons pushing on past the obstacles in life. Other notable beers that weather the Fort Myers heat in the brewery are Gateway Golden Honey Blonde, a sweet and malty 6 percent blonde ale; City of Palms Pale Ale, the approachable and citrusy pale ale; and the Cypress Strong Ale, coming at 9.3 percent alcohol and very sweet with some spicy notes on the finish. Rob has several other recipes he is working through as the brewery gets its sea legs and navigates the tides in the City of Palms and tries to keep up with local demand.

The locals are certainly on to something: Fort Myers Brewing continues to pack the house on weekends and is moving through batches very quickly for a brewery that is still in its toddler years. If Lee County's welcoming embrace is any indication, Fort Myers Brewing will have to expand again in the near future. Next time the compass points to southwest Florida or riding the ferry to Key West, Fort Myers now has a brewery to provide one for the watery road to the Conch Republic.

The Mack House

Brewery/Tasting Room
9118 State Road 84, Fort Lauderdale 33324
(954) 474-5040
http://themackhouse.com
Closed Monday

The Mack House is the tasting room for one of Florida's premiere Belgian-inspired ales, Holy Mackerel. The Mack House serves as the epicenter of Holy Mackerel beers and gives Holy Mackerel's brewers a place to do treatments on their beers as well as make small test batches for research and development. It is located in a strip mall in the Fort Lauderdale/Davie area, so look for the sign that says "BREWERY" to find the treasure buried in Fort Lauderdale, six miles from the airport and just off the Port Everglades Expressway.

The Mack House is the next phase in the evolution of Holy Mackerel Beers, the company founded by brewer Bobby Gordash to distribute his Belgian-inspired beers that began in his home brewery, minutes away from the tasting room. Gordash has been brewing for twenty years, and was selected as one of the winners of Samuel Ad-

ams's Longshot Homebrew Competition in 1996. Samuel Adams, under the Longshot Label, then bottled Gordash's beer, and Gordash also received a trip to Europe as a prize from the competition. The victory inspired him to begin thinking about opening his own brewery, and spawned the fish-themed brewery from there. Because Gordash did not have a brewery at the time, the Holy Mackerel was a contract-brewed beer out of the Florida Beer Company in Melbourne. While the bottles and kegs are now brewed on a large scale in South Carolina at Thomas Creek Brewery, the Mack House serves as the primary facility for Holy Mackerel. Bobby Gordash exited Holy Mackerel in June of 2013, and the company continues under investor and manager Larry Hetfield and family.

Inside the Mack House lies a cozy tasting room and brewery that houses Holy Mackerel's two core beers, Special Golden Ale and Panic Attack, along with the in-and-out seasonal Mack In Black—the roasty stout infused with pomegranate. All of Holy Mackerel's beers make the drinker say that very phrase, as the Belgian-inspired ales pack quite a wallop, both in flavor and in alcohol content. Holy Mackerel Special Golden stands at 8.5 percent alcohol, Mack In Black reports 8 percent alcohol, and Panic Attack registers a whopping 10 percent alcohol on the craft beer Richter Scale. While Special Golden and Panic Attack are always on draft at Mack House, the nanobrewery onsite also has a fifty-five-gallon yield that allows the brewery to pour test batches of beer like Wormwood Stout, a stout brewed with the namesake root, or Panic Con Pablo, a roasted coffee treatment of Panic Attack that displays remarkable sweetness as the sweet Belgian ale and roasted coffee dance a tango in the glass. If the Holy Mackerel is between beers, then expect other Florida breweries to be displayed at the Mack House while a concert is going on or a charity event is happening.

The Mack House is a nice place to see an intimate concert of live music, hang out and discuss beers with friends, or see what the brewery's latest concoction might be. This oasis in the beating heart of the city is looking to be a true Florida craft beer bar showcasing craft beer from all over the state, including some house beers that are not poured from anyone else's taps.

Organic Brewery

Brewpub
290 North Broadwalk, Hollywood 33019
(305) 414-4757
http://organicbreweryhollywood.com
Hours: Noon to midnight, daily

While other breweries in South Florida hold geographic distinctions, Hollywood's Organic Brewery might be the one closest to the Atlantic Ocean. Other breweries can boast a close proximity, but the prettiest green-blue ocean view of any brewery is visible from Organic Brewery's front porch. The brewery shelters a German-style biergarten right in the middle of a very touristy boardwalk area of Hollywood, Florida, on the northern outskirts of Miami.

People who visit Hollywood's gorgeous beaches sustain Organic Brewery. The environment is very laid-back and people can meander from lying on the sand to standing at the bar in a matter of feet. After all, anyone who is on Hollywood's beach is either staying local or staying for a while—so a beach brewery is ideally suited for the South Florida sea breeze lifestyle.

Once inside the brewery, the brewing equipment is visible from all points and the bustling barkeep can pour one of many beers that rotate through the brewery's taps. The brewery endeavors to keep eight organic beers on draft at any given time. The main beers include a mean-looking stout called Russian Knight, a lightly sweet German pilsner, a fruity Belgian ale, and a biscuity British IPA. From the core four, the remaining four taps rotate with the beer that the spirit best moves the brewer toward.

Organic Brewery waters (or beers, as applicable) people parched from the brilliant South Florida sun and sand. A few bricks worth of distance and a parking meter or condo rental are all that stand between anyone and one of Organic Brewery's beers.

Insider Tip: Parking is difficult for this brewery. The best idea is to park in a garage or the first available space. It is not uncommon to make over a dozen laps around the beach to find a space.

Saltwater Brewing Company

Brewery
1701 West Atlantic Avenue, Delray Beach 33444
(561) 865-5373
Open 7 days a week

Saltwater Brewing Company is a brewery with a vision beyond the beer: a family whose heart is set on helping the ocean and whose vision has inspired others to work with the brewery. Leigh Gove and his sons shared a vision of opening a brewery in the old farmhouse that the Goves had owned for 15 years. Many family and friends lent their hands and expertise to the Gove family in the building of Saltwater Brewery, with the final piece of the puzzle coming on a trip to Montana, where Peter Agardy, a childhood friend was on a fishing trip. Peter went to a local brewery and after sampling the beers met Bill Taylor, a Montana brewer who wanted an excuse to move to Florida and work with a startup brewery. As all the pieces fell into place, the brewery began to move toward construction and opening day.

Saltwater Brewery is located off I-95 in the town of Delray Beach, which is south of Boynton Beach and north of Coral Springs/Alligator Alley. The brewery is housed in a 7,880–square-foot, two-story farmhouse, built in the mid-1900s, a historical building that used to house Delray Beach Farm Supply. The tasting room holds the brewery's thirty-two-foot bar, home to twenty-two tap handles of Saltwater and Florida beer. The brewery staff has tried to save, restore, and use as much of the historic material from the old farmhouse as possible, including many pieces of Dade County pine. The brewery sits adjacent to the railroad in Delray Beach, a combination of history, atmosphere, and sea air.

Saltwater's beers illustrate the brewery's mission of conservation: all beers are named for sea life. Saltwater Brewery brews on a twenty-barrel brewhouse and a five-gallon pilot brewing system. The brewery has six beers in its starting lineup: South End Session Ale, a summer-loving beer that is low in alcohol and high in hop flavor; Screamin' Reels IPA, a West Coast–style IPA that is assertive in hoppiness; Stinger Double IPA, an imperial IPA for the hop lover, named for the pesky stinging jellyfish that lurk off Florida's shores; Sea Cow Milk Stout, this roasty stout is more named for the depths of mystery; Bonafide Blonde Belgian Blonde Ale, a light ale with a fruity Belgian yeast; and malty, strong, and high-gravity Flying Scotsman Scotch Ale.

Saltwater Brewery's beers are soon available in South Florida, and its tasting room and tropical beer garden are a sight to behold and currently the only place to try a saltwater brew.

Sailfish Brewing Company

Brewery
407 North Second Street, Fort Pierce 34950
(772) 242-8697
http://www.sailfishbrewingco.com
Closed Monday and Tuesday

Sailfish Brewing Company was begotten by the need for fresh beer in the sailfish capital of the world. Three friends saw a need and renovated a house in order to fill it. That house would be transformed into Sailfish Brewing Company—making small batches of beer in order to aid the fisherman's call for craft beer and assist in the catch of many (proverbial) blue marlins and provide Fort Pierce's mariners with liquid refreshment.

Sailfish Brewing Company charted a course when two friends decided to open a brewery. Owners Dave BuShea and Nick Bischoff worked together to find the resources to open the brewery and pulled in another friend to brew the beers for them. Since Fort Pierce and Stuart hold the title of Sailfish Capital of the World and the friends shared a mutual love of fishing, the name seemed to fit like a tallboy in a can koozie. Fort Pierce was founded as a town on the sea: its ports were gateways to the open ocean, and fishing was a huge business until the hurricanes of 2003 came through and damaged the industry. The area has begun to see reinvestment from the city, and like the city, the brewery hopes to grow as more people embrace Florida's east coast. Dave and Nick began working with local officials to rewrite city codes to allow for a local brewery (and an oyster bar next door). The guys then began promoting their beers at local festivals on Florida's east coast, the Sailfish Brewery's maiden voyage began on April 6, 2013, opening doors and taps to Fort Pierce. Sailfish quickly attracted the attention of North Carolina brewer Kevin Storm, who took the wheel and headed up Sailfish's brewing operations into the future.

The Treasure Coast's first craft brewery has invested in a small thirty-five-gallon brewing system to produce quality core beers and local favorites. Sailfish set out to make approachable and drinkable beers that will allow land sharks a short ferry into the world of artisan ales and craft brewing. While the guys look forward to brewing all manner of beers—ones that they care for as well as ones the public will embrace—the core lineup is developing, but the citrusy and approachable Pelagic Pale Ale will anchor the line; followed by Tag and Release Amber Ale, a malty and mildly spicy amber ale with a small amount of rye; finished by Sunrise City IPA, an IPA whose citrus bite could bend a line or two and would pair well with a sunrise fishing trip or marinate the catch of the day. Aside from the mainline beers, expect to see rotating seasonals and research beers while the brewery develops, beers like the Mariana Trench

Saison—a Belgian-inspired heavy-hitter at 10 percent alcohol, and the White Marlin Wheat, whose light, bready character and 5 percent alcohol presence allow for fishing stories and long-term anchoring.

Sailfish Brewing Company is not just a fishing story; the beers are flowing and distribution along the Treasure Coast should follow suit shortly. While Sailfish might currently be a destination brewery, it can easily be a day trip with a straight shot up or down I-95. Sailfish has become part of east Florida's craft beer corridor.

Point Ybel Brewing Company

Brewery
16120 San Carlos Boulevard, Fort Myers 33908
(239) 603-6535
http://www.pointybelbrew.com
Open 7 days a week

Former fishing guide Walter Costello is poised to direct the sunny folks of South Florida in a new way: showing them the way to hand-crafted beer. He directed locals to Point Ybel Brewing Company, named for the part of Sanibel Island that housed the first lighthouse north of Key West, marking the entrance to San Carlos Bay. Costello, a six-year home brewer, opened Point Ybel Brewing Company to distribute local craft beer to Sanibel Island and surrounding areas.

While construction delays kept postponing the opening of the Hurricane Hole, Point Ybel's tasting room, and preventing Costello from brewing beers for Point Ybel, Walt never lost heart. Encouraged by the camaraderie and collaborative spirit of southwest Florida, Costello persevered, and on September 17, 2013, the day finally arrived for Costello to brew his first batch of Snook Bite Red Ale at Point Ybel. Local brewers and home brewers came and assisted Walt as he mashed, boiled, and pitched. Progress continued until opening day, December 14, 2013.

Point Ybel brews on a four-barrel brewing system and produces four core beers: Endless Summer Pale Ale, a 5.5 percent alcohol citrus and tropical fruity pale ale; Sanibel Red Island Ale, a red ale that shows off bready and toasted malt character made with local mangrove honey; Snook Bite IPA, a balanced IPA that boasts five hop varietals utilized in brewing, the mysterious Black Mangrove American Dark Ale; and finally the local ingredient-conscious Yay! Sanibel Saison, a saison made with key lime zest, orange blossom honey, and bird pepper. Costello also maintains a small half-barrel pilot system to perfect recipes and test brew new ideas.

Point Ybel's beers are on draft in the South Florida market, with the Hurricane Hole and southwest Florida getting the freshest selection.

Marco Island Brewery

Brewpub
1089 North Collier Boulevard, Marco Island 34145
(239) 970-0461
http://www.marcoislandbrewery.com
Open 7 days a week

Marco Island Brewery is a brewpub on Marco Island, the farthest southwestern point on mainland Florida. The brewpub has an antique feel with dark wood and vintage cars (and a nice-looking truck parked directly in front). Father-and-son team Frank and John LaCava own Marco Island Brewery; the pub's doors opened in September of 2010.

The restaurant offers indoor and outdoor seating and the brewing tanks are visible from any point in the corner-of-the-plaza pub. While Marco Island Brewery is not directly on the water, the bay breezes are not far from the patio on any given afternoon. Marco Island's beers run the gamut of style and color: beginning with a lightly hopped, fruity Pelican Pilsner and moving to a lightly malty amber ale dubbed Loggerhead Red, on to an Earthy English IPA called The Rock, and finally to a spiced winter stout for the pseudo-cold of tropical southwest Florida.

The brewpub has plans to distribute offsite, but at present the only place for Marco Island's beers is at the brewpub.

MIA Brewing Company

Brewery
10400 Northwest 33rd Street, Suite 150, Miami 33172
(305) 567-5550
http://www.MIAbrewing.com

MIA Brewing Company's eyes have been set on the Doral area of Miami for a while now. The brewery began its life as an idea in the mind of owner Eddie Leon as Most Wanted Brewery, but due to some minor trademark disagreements with a distillery that makes Most Wanted Vodka, the brewery changed its name to MIA Brewing Company. The Wild West theme is carried on in MIA, which still makes beers with the outlaw/Wild West naming scheme despite the loss of the Most Wanted moniker.

MIA Brewing brews on a twenty-barrel brewhouse and has five core beers. The first is a light hefeweizen known as High Noon Sweet Orange Hefeweizen—this one permeates flavors of sweet citrus and light fruit character. Next is Pink Posse, a hibiscus and floral ale followed by Crimin Ale, a honey wheat beer that cements MIA's outlaw theme. On the bitter side of the spectrum is Hops and Robbers and on the dark and stout side is Smokin' Barrel Chicory Black Porter.

Most Wanted Beverages, a distributorship that is loosely affiliated with the brewery, will distribute MIA Brewing's products in South Florida.

Bone Island Brewing Company

Brewery
1111 Eaton Street, Key West 33040
(305) 304-3472
http://www.facebook.com/boneislandbrewing
Closed Sunday

Bone Island Brewing Company is one of the Conch Republic's newest craft breweries. Brewer Jim Brady is looking to make the best possible beer he can while staying true to beer style in his small brewery.

Jim Brady is using his twenty years of home brewing experience to guide Bone Island, brewing at home before the Florida Keys even had a distributor to bring beer that far south. Brady is both a Cicerone and a Certified Beer Judge, skills he uses in consumer education, after all, Brady says, "I want my visitors to be brutally honest about my offerings. Politely placating me had no value. It goes back to my belief that there's always room for improvement." Brady's resume includes some credentials distinctly from Key West, he has been appointed as the Conch Republic Ambassador to Ninkasi (the ancient Sumerian beer goddess) by Sir Peter Anderson, Secretary General of the Conch Republic. As one of the most recent feathers in Brady's hat, in 2013 he was awarded the John Doble III Brewing Scholarship by the Florida Brewers' Guild and completed a course in brewing science at the Siebel Institute of Brewing Science in Chicago.

Bone Island Brewing is named for Cayo Hueso, the old Spanish name for Key West and seeks to brew all manner of ales, and lagers eventually, on his small but fierce one-point-seven barrel brewing system. Brady is a fan of history, science, and beer, so he incorporates them all into his brewing repertoire. Bone Island's core beers illustrate Brady's eclectic passions. Bone Island's stalwart core beers are Black Hole Oatmeal Stout, Benediction Belgian Tripel, Velvet Lace Belgian Witbier, Hefe El Jefe Hefeweizen, and Richard's Burton Pale Ale (the storefront owner's name is Richard, and this is an English Pale Ale in the style of Burton-Upon-Trent). Each beer traces its name and recipe to both the Florida Keys and Brady's love of science and history combining Spanish influence, beer stories, and unique names to forge a unique set of beers.

Insider Tip: Brady reserves the right to substitute any beers in his lineup for a pilot beer or a beer from his "Black Hole Series" that includes Event Horizon Porter and/or the Singularity Stout aged on vanilla and bourbon barrel oak.

BREWERIES IN FERMENTATION

While many areas of Florida keep sprouting new craft breweries, South Florida (especially Miami and the Florida Keys) is an area that is on the verge of an eruption. See for yourself how many breweries are currently in the hopper.

Gravity Brewlab

Gravity Brewlab has been several years in the making by owners Diego Ganoza and Luigi Cantanzaro. Gravity has been trying to establish itself around Florida by making consistent festival appearances and has been trying to secure a location for several years. Gravity makes some extremely creative beers and, like a secret admirer, has had its eyes set on the city of Miami for a while. Once Gravity's ship comes in, it will be a boon to the Magic City, as another in a line of flavorful ales.

Fourth Age Brewing Company

Home brewers Chris Campos and Danny Morales have been buzzing around Miami getting the word out about their new brewery. As two teachers who are looking to become brewers, Fourth Age wants to stand out in the rising tide of Miami craft breweries. The two friends have begun their journey to breweryship with a fan favorite Flan Stout along with beers brewed with tropical and Florida fruit like kiwi, mango, and blueberry. Look for more information from Fourth Age as the owners lock down a location and continue to make their mark on the Miami area.

Florida Keys Brewing Company

Florida Keys Brewing Company is the result of the growth of home brewer Craig McBay into a commercial brewer. Florida Keys Brewing Company will be housed in Islamorada in the keys, and will feature a fifteen-barrel brewing system. Craig and his wife, Cheryl, are planning a brewery and tasting room to highlight their Flakeys Key Lime Witbier, Run-a-Ground Brown Ale, and Honey-Bottomed Blonde Ale, among others.

The Waterfront Brewery

The Waterfront Brewery is a brewery in development in Key West. The brewery has posted pictures of demolition taking place at its 201 William Street facility.

Fat Point Brewing Company

The craft beer industry is replete with stories of people quitting lucrative jobs to enjoy a life brewing beer. Fat Point Brewing owner, Bill Frazier, left a job in the automotive industry to pursue crafting his own beer in South Florida. In the Punta Gorda area, Frazier was interested in running Beecher Brewing Company as a brewpub. After the move to Punta Gorda, he decided to change the name to Fat Point Brewing Company in honor of the brewpub's new home. Frazier then put down a deposit on a fifteen-barrel brewing system and began construction on the Punta Gorda location, a 12,000-square-foot location in Charlotte County.

Coppertop Brewing Company

Coppertop Brewing Company is an emerging craft brewery in development currently looking for a space to call home in the Delray Beach area.

Three Horns Brewing Company

Three Horns Brewing is a brewery under consideration and development in the Lake Worth area of Florida.

Opus Ales

Opus Ales is a brewery in development in Hallandale Beach by three home brewers. Their brewing mission is to introduce Florida to the flavors of the Caribbean, South American, and Central American ingredients.

Concrete Beach Brewery

Concrete Beach Brewery, an offshoot of the Sam Adams investment known as Alchemy and Science, began construction on a brewery in the Wynwood neighborhood of Miami in October of 2013. It should be both a brewery and a tasting room with bottle releases into the community and draft offerings at the brewery.

3 Sons Brewing Company

3 Sons Brewing Company is a brewery in planning in the Davie area. The brewers have visited Saint Petersburg to collaborate with Brewers' Tasting Room on several beers and are currently working on details for their brewery.

Barrel of Monks Brewing Company

Working with a twenty-barrel brewing system, Barrel of Monks Brewing Company is brewing at 1141 South Rogers Circle in Boca

Raton; its motto is "Serious beers for people who don't take themselves too seriously."

LauderAle

LauderAle is a brewery in planning in the Fort Lauderdale area. The LauderAle project began in 2013 with the idea of perfecting recipes and ingredients and becoming Fort Lauderdale's first craft brewery.

Bury Me Brewing

Bury Me Brewing is a brewery in planning on Gulf Center Drive in Fort Myers. The brewery applied for its brewers permits, and as of February 2014, it was still waiting on word from the federal government.

6

Florida Contract Breweries

Florida currently has several craft breweries that do not have their own facilities. These contract beers are brewed at existing breweries, bottled or kegged, and then marketed to the community at large. For many breweries, this is one small step on the path to a larger business. For others, this is a necessary step into the business while establishing their brand. For some, it is a way to get business before they can brew beer on their own.

Orange Blossom Brewing Company

Contract Beer
https://www.facebook.com/obpbeer

Owner Tom Moench has been a part of Florida's beer industry since 1993 and Orange Blossom Pilsner, or OBP, is his third foray into beer as a business. Moench had a beer equipment company and a small distributorship, both of which he sold to former partners. He then focused his attention on Orange Blossom Pilsner full time.

OBP currently has three brands of beer in bottles, all brewed at South Carolina's Thomas Creek Brewery. The proverbial ox that built the house is Orange Blossom Pilsner, a light and lightly sweet pilsner, finishing at 5.5 percent alcohol. Moench tweaked OBP's recipe as a home brewer. After rave reviews he released it as a commercial beer in 1999. OBP took home a bronze medal from the Great American Beer Festival in 2004 in the Specialty Honey Ale or Lager category. Later came OBP Squared, the pilsner's older and heftier sibling, finishing at 11 percent alcohol, and as the website pegs it: "Half the Water, Twice the Flavor." Squared has a much stronger honey presence and a pronounced, almost cloying sweetness. Finally, at 5.25 percent alcohol Orange Blossom Pilsner's lightest beer is also its darkest: Toasted Coconut Porter showcases notes of chocolate, roasted malt, and coconut in its light and roasty body. Toasted Coconut Porter was established and released in December 2011.

According to an article in the Orlando Business Journal from 2011, OBP is available on tap in sixty locations around Florida and in bottles at over three hundred locations. OBP's beers are available in Florida, North Carolina, South Carolina, Alabama, and Tennessee.

The next step for OBP is to open a full production brewery. In late 2013, Orange Blossom Pilsner transitioned to Orange Blossom Brewing Company and began brewing beer at Rookie's Pub in Brooksville (formerly the Saint Sebastian Brewery). Not long after beginning with Rookie's, Orange Blossom Brewing signed a contract with The Brew Hub in Lakeland to brew beer at its new facility.

Inlet Brewing Company

Contract Beer
P.O. Box 1483, Jupiter 33468
http://www.inletbrewing.com

Inlet Brewing Company is a small contract operation that has its beer brewed at Thomas Creek Brewery in South Carolina. Inlet

Brewing began with one beer on the market called Monk in the Trunk.

Inlet's main beer, Monk in the Trunk, is an amber ale fermented with a Belgian yeast. Monk in the Trunk is amber in color, and the Belgian yeast fills the aroma with fruitiness as well as some light nutty notes from the malt. Monk in the Trunk also uses organic hops in its brewing, making this beer as organic as possible, and at 5 percent alcohol by volume, Monk in the Trunk is very drinkable in both hot season and not-as-hot season.

In late 2013, Inlet Brewing released Monk IPA in bottles to join Monk in the Trunk, working as a pair to slake Florida's thirst.

Monk in the Trunk and Monk IPA are available in Central and South Florida in bottles and occasionally on draft.

Holy Mackerel Beers

Contract Beer
902 Southwest 8th Street, Fort Lauderdale 33315
http://www.holymackerelbeers.com/

Holy Mackerel Beers are the concoctions of owner/brewer Bobby Gordash and are commonly distributed throughout the state of Florida, contract brewed at Thomas Creek Brewery in South Carolina. Gordash won the Samuel Adams Longshot Homebrew Contest in 1996 for his Extra Special Bitter, and his accolades and love for Belgian beer helped carry him and Holy Mackerel to its current status.

Holy Mackerel has three core beers, and they are all relatively high in alcohol. The fish that built the boat is the Special Golden Ale, strong, fruity, and bold at 8.5 percent alcohol. The next beer that Gordash developed was a three-way hybrid of an imperial stout, a Belgian ale, and a fruit beer in Mack in Black. Mack in Black is the quiet one, in a "no one puts Baby in a corner" kind of way—8 percent alcohol. The newest addition to the school of Mack is the big and sweet Panic Attack Golden Ale. Panic Attack is a full 10 percent alcohol and its fruity and spicy sweet qualities are best enjoyed while sipping. For full details, see the listing of The Mack House in Fort Lauderdale, where Holy Mackerel Beers serves its lineup as well as one-off beers brewed on-site.

Holy Mackerel beers are available in bottles and on draft throughout the entire state of Florida.

Rock Brothers Brewing Company

Contract Beer

Rock Brothers is a company that pairs artists from the music industry with brewers from the beer industry and lets the collaboration commence. Much like developing the ensemble in songwriting, the brewers and musicians craft a recipe that will accentuate and appeal to a craft audience.

Rock Brothers' first collaboration was a beer designed for the Bradenton-based band Have Gun, Will Travel and was named High Road Ale, after a song on the band's album *Fiction, Fact, or Folktale?* Cigar City Brewer Josh Brengle designed the beer to remind folks of the band's hometown of Bradenton and the local Tropicana Plant. Brengle used the aromatic qualities of several hops from New Zealand and the Pacific Islands to make a citrus-forward pale ale, and High Road Pale Ale went on to win the National Grand Championship at the U.S. Beer Tasting Championship, taking top honors away from a field of competition amongst hundreds of other beers from around the United States.

The second band to sign with Rock Brothers is J. J. Grey, whose beer will be designed in collaboration with both Cigar City Brewing and Saint Petersburg's Green Bench Brewing Company.

Rock Brothers' beers are available in the home market of the artist that they collaborated with and in Rock Brothers' market.

Froghair Beer Company

Contract Beer

Froghair Beer Company has designed one beer, its core beer, that the owners feel pairs well with the game of golf: Froghair Blonde Ale. At 5 percent alcohol by volume, the refreshing and citrusy ale is great for the Florida outdoors. Froghair is named for the fringe around the green in the game of golf, and seeks to be the first choice in golf course beer.

Froghair is brewed by Pensacola Bay Brewery and is distributed in the Tampa Bay area and beyond, focusing primarily on golf courses' tap rooms and some fine craft beer bars.

Brew Bus Brewing Company

Contract Beer

Brew Bus Brewing Company is part of the Tampa Bay Brew Bus, soon to become The Brew Bus. It all began when Tampa Bay Brew Bus founder Toni Derby looked to Cigar City Brewing to help brew a beer that would be a unique part of the experience of riding on the Tampa Bay Brew Bus—an exclusive beer to enjoy on bus rides. As the Brew Bus business began to expand, so too did the offerings.

Brew Bus brewing began with one core beer: Rollin' Dirty Red Ale. Rollin' Dirty is a malty and mildly bitter beer with low alcohol content that would allow riders to enjoy several beers during a long trip. Next came Are Wheat There Yet? a citrusy, hoppy wheat ale that gave riders another option if they were not fond of malty beers. After bottling the two core beers for several months, Brew Bus Brewing decided to expand its offerings to Last Stop IPA and You're My Boy Blue, Blueberry Ale and quickly moved all of its beers into cans.

Brew Bus is working on a series of wood-aged beers to accompany its regular lineup. Cedar-aged Rollin' Dirty is the lead-off hitter in that series. In addition, Brew Bus Brewing is adding a porter to its can lineup.

Brew Bus Brewing's beers are brewed at Cigar City Brewing and are available throughout the state of Florida in cans and kegs.

Ya Kilt It Brewing

Contract Beer

Ya Kilt It Brewing is another Florida contract brewery that focuses on golf courses and their "19th Hole" Tap Rooms. The beer came from owner Wayne Lutz's desire to play golf with his friends and drink well-crafted beer while doing so.

Ya Kilt It Brewing has one core beer with three other beers in development. The beer that tees it up is called Dog Leg Ale, a citrusy pale ale that is meant to pair well with an afternoon of golf. Under construction are One Putt Pils, Albatross English IPA, and Swing Lube Stout.

Ya Kilt It's beers are available in Central Florida.

Native Brewing Company

Contract Beer

Native Brewing Company is a contract brewery that began with native Floridian Adam Fine trying to develop great beer specifically suited for his home state.

Native Brewing Company fine-tuned recipes until each of the three beers in the portfolio were under 5.3 percent alcohol. Native's three core beers include the crisp, German-style lager dubbed Native Lager. The beer that Native began with was a 4.2 percent alcohol brown ale called The Eleven. The name actually comes from the numbering on the first bottle when Fine was moving through recipes for possible beers; he preferred the batch in bottle number eleven most of all, and the name stuck. With a light alcohol presence and the flavor of caramel and a touch of roasted nuts, The Eleven is as Florida as beaches and bathing suits. The final beer in Native's bag of tricks is Thunderhead Red, named for Florida's quick-moving afternoon storms. This easygoing amber has a bit of caramel in the malt and some mild bitterness and a smile. Native Brewing is also working on a new addition to the lineup with a hoppy pale ale called Glades Pale Ale in addition to a Glades IPA and various other beer styles as Native transitions from contract brewing to starting a small brewery.

Native Brewing Company's beers are available in bottles and on draft in South Florida, from Tequesta to Key West.

Fantasy Brewmasters

Contract Beer

Fantasy Brewmasters, maker of Burdisson's Dwarven Ale, bases its business out of Naples. Fantasy Brewmasters brews beers inspired by "the epic realms of dwarves, dragons, and magic." The company is run by its founder, Chris Guerra, and the beers are currently contract brewed at Butternuts beer in New York.

Burdisson's Dwarven Ale is the first offering from Fantasy, and Guerra is currently seeking to expand his lineup, possibly into an IPA.

GRATITUDE

For their assistance and encouragement, I owe a debt of gratitude to the following individuals.

Three individuals played major roles in helping this book become a reality. The first was my lovely and loving wife, Carrie, whose patience and push helped spur me onward. She put up with me and my "hobby," always encouraging and never letting me surrender this project until I saw it through. For that you have my gratitude, my faith, and my abiding love. You give so much more than you ask for. Thank you, love. Sunrays and Saturdays.

Next is Maurice "Socky" O'Sullivan, who when I approached him about this book as an idea for a master's thesis told me it was a great idea. We kind of lost touch, but I hope he knows how much he helped. Finally, Joseph J. M. Redner provided insight, counseling, a kick in the butt, and a threat to write the book himself if I didn't hurry up. He wrote the foreword.

Marty and Jan Cummins generously provided a traveling writer grant for me in the spring of 2005. I am eternally grateful for the trip to Key West that taught me about the discipline, the fire, and the beauty of writing.

Justin Clark also provided countless phone calls of help. To him, I am very grateful.

I gratefully acknowledge the generous donation of time given by Dale Swope, Cortney Curtis, Andy Huse, Wayne Wambles, Richard Gonzmart, Byron Burroughs, Bob Sylvester, Brian and Kelly Fenstermacher, David Doble, Michael Wagner, Doug Dozark, Tim Ogden, Geiger Powell, Michael Zane, Ben Davis, Todd Strauss, Johnathan Wakefield, Jennifer Dietz, Ron Raike, Ryan Sentz, Kevin Abbot, Will Lawson, Steve Halford, Eric Luman, Paul Evans, Kent Waugh, Tom Barris, Clay Yarn, Bishop, Matt Manthe, Mike Bryant, Sky Conley, John Cheek, Mike Halker, Jay Dingman, Matt Abdoney, Larry Hatfield, Aaron Nesbit, Elliot Eckland, Mark Robertson, Randy Reaver, Luke Kemper, Andy Bielecki, Craig Birkmaier, Tony Falso, Greg Rapp, Fran Andrewlevitch, Bruce Talcott, Doug Murr, Vance Joy, Scott Bannester, Donny Dye, Luch Scremin, Nick Bischoff, Dave BuShea, Rob Whyte, Donna Copp, Khris Johnson, Ken and Julia Rosenthal, Luis Brignoni, Mike Harting, and the countless others who showed this traveling writer some kindness or the grace of their time.

Ratebeer.com, its founder Joe Tucker, and fellow beer writer Ken Weaver also provided me with a treasure trove of resources, including their expertise and guidance. To them, I am truly grateful.

Actor Nathan Fillion helped by portraying Malcolm Reynolds in the series *Firefly*. Mal always found a way to do (almost all) the things that were important in life, and kept his friends close. Ceaselessly loyal to friends and not letting anyone get in his way, the character was a good example of following the right stars through the maelstrom of the universe toward daring goals.

I would be remiss if I did not thank Sian Hunter and the fine folks at University Press of Florida/Seaside Publishing for their faith and help with this book.

Also, my thanks to the many historical societies and universities whose doorsteps I darkened. I am in your debt. Statewide, Florida is a state with magnificent librarians, the most magnificent of whom I worked with at Saint Leo University's library; to Darla Asher, you had no idea what all those brewery articles were for, and I hope this explains it.

This book also benefited from the friendship, expertise, and unstinting advice of people like Allen Espinosa, Tony Gonzalez, Ross Appel, and Emily Komlossy.

Finally, to the Tampa Tasting Group whose support and questions of "How's the book going?" kept me pushing onward: Paul Unwin, Jason Carter, Matt Rego, Dave Franich, Greg Cotner, Sebastien Jadot, Gary Kost, Shawn Shaut, Adam Wintenburg, Eric Starnes, Danny Rowland, and John Watts. Cheers, guys!

FLORIDA BEER
TIMELINE

1824	Fort Brooke (military outpost on Tampa Bay) established.
1857	Milwaukee, Wisconsin, reports that over 100,000 barrels of beer are brewed by brewers in that city.
Fall 1885	Vincente Martinez Ybor leaves Key West to move operations to Tampa.
1896	Construction begins on Florida Brewing Company (Tampa).
1896	Miami is incorporated as a city.
February 15, 1897	Florida Brewing Company (Tampa) formally opens; throws opening party.
February 1899	Florida Brewing Company begins sending beer to Cuba.
1901	The Great Fire of Jacksonville destroys 2,368 buildings in Jacksonville.
June 1909	Florida Brewing Company suffers $30,000 in damages from Ybor City Fire.

1911	Florida Brewing Company adds $30,000 worth of improvements to property.
June 9, 1913	Ground is broken on the Jacksonville Brewing Company.
May 6, 1914	The first Jax beer hits the market.
1918	1,000 breweries operating nationwide.
May 4, 1918	The city of Jacksonville votes to become completely dry, banning alcohol sales.
January 17, 1920	The Volstead Act takes effect; period of Prohibition begins.
1920	National brewery count is only 500 still operating.
March 22, 1933	The Cullen-Harrison Act signed, 3.2 percent ABV legalized; beer can be made and sold again.
May 8, 1933	Florida legalizes 3.2 percent beer again (lagging behind nation because Florida legislature refuses to vote earlier).
May 20, 1933	Jax Brewery is first Florida beer to return to market after Prohibition.
November 28, 1933	Florida Brewing Company (Tampa) returns beer to market after Prohibition as Tampa Florida Brewery, Inc.
December 5, 1933	The 21st Amendment is passed, thus ending national Prohibition.
April 6, 1934	Miami Breweries (and those in planning) form the Florida Brewers' Association.
July 1, 1934	Flamingo Brewing Company's beers hit Miami shelves.

January 1935	Western Brewer Magazine advertises Flamingo Brewing for sale.
February 5, 1935	Jax Brewery is able to pay off all debts.
1939	Jax Brewery sells 35,000 barrels of beer.
1943	Jax Brewery sells 103,048 barrels of beer.
1954	The price of a can of Jax beer is reduced to 20 cents, 5 cents below national brands.
1955	Atlantic Brewing Company of Orlando closes its doors.
August 31, 1956	Jax Brewery sells brewing equipment and exists as a cold storage facility.
1956	Erwin Uihlein breaks ground on a plant for Schlitz Brewing that would become 11111 N. 30th Street in Tampa.
1958	211 beermakers are operating 252 plants making beer nationwide.
1958	Anheuser Busch buys 160 acres a half-mile from the Tampa Schlitz facility with plans to build a $20 million facility.
1967	Fritz Maytag buys Anchor Brewing.
1973	Schlitz Brewing admits to using corn syrup and hop extracts to decrease supply prices.
Winter 1974	Regal Brewery of Miami closes its doors.
1977	McGuire's Irish Pub opens in Pensacola, Florida.
October 1, 1983	Schlitz sells Tampa plant to Pabst Brewing for $8.5 million.
1987	McGuire's Irish Pub of Pensacola adds a brewery to the existing pub.

March 1, 1988	Pabst sells Tampa plant to Stroh Brewing for $6.4 million.
1989	Hops brewpub founders establish a brewery and pub in Clearwater.
1994	Ybor City Brewing Company begins operations.
1996	Doble family opens Tampa Bay Brewing Company brewpub.
1996	Bryant family opens Dunedin Brewery in Dunedin.
1997	McGuire's Irish Pub and Brewery of Destin opens its doors.
April 1, 1999	Stroh Brewing sells Tampa plant to Yuengling Brewery for $6 million.
2000	Ybor City Brewing Company closes its doors.

NOTES

Chapter 1. The Earliest Florida Brew: Brewing in Tampa

Page 7   This man, Eduardo Manrara . . . : Tony Pizzo, "Eduardo Manrara The Cigar Manufacturing Prince of the Nation," *Sunland Tribune,* October, 1975.

Page 7   Manrara was fifty-four years old . . . : Glenn Westfall, *Don Vincente Martinez Ybor, The Man and His Empire* (New York: Garland Publishing, 1987), 159.

Page 8   They would pay a saloon owner's mortgage . . . : Frank Alduino, "The 'Noble Experiment' in Tampa: A Study of Prohibition in Urban America" (Ann Arbor, MI: UMI Dissertation Services, 1989), 77–78.

Page 9   Having established offices in Key West . . . : "Tampa's Pride—The Only Brewery in Florida," *Tampa Tribune,* Midwinter Edition, 1900.

Page 10   For this celebration . . . : "Come and Celebrate," *Tampa Tribune,* February 13, 1897.

Page 10   At the end of the day, twenty carcasses . . . : Kip Sharpe, "The Tampa Florida Brewery, Inc. Florida's First Brewery," *Sunland Tribune,* November 1992.

Page 11   "The consequence of [owning . . ." : Archive, University of South Florida, Collection?, St. Petersburg

Page 12   According to brewing journals . . . : *The Western Brewer,* October 1898.

Page 12   Soon after Tampa's beer . . . : *American Breweriana Journal*, November/December 1985.

Page 12   . . . virtually all of the bottled beer . . . : Alduino, "The 'Noble Experiment' in Tampa," 80.

Page 12   As the city was getting its first street lights . . . : Gary Mormino, *The Immigrant World of Ybor City: Italians and Their Latin Neighbors* (Gainesville: University Press of Florida, 1998), 50.

Page 13   One prominent Prohibitionist . . . : Alduino, "The 'Noble Experiment,'" 23.

Page 13   In a referendum . . . : ibid., 72.

Page 14   "In order to have a chance . . .": ibid., 136.

Page 15   Wall would have had more of a need . . . : *The Brewer's Journal*, May 1909.

Page 15   "The Columbia's bartenders . . .": Andrew Huse, *The Columbia Restaurant: Celebrating a Century of History, Culture, and Cuisine* (Gainesville: University Press of Florida, 2009), 10.

Page 16   A New Orleans appellate court . . . : Kip, "Florida's First," 7.

Page 16   Once that accusation . . . : Frank Alduino, "Prohibition in Tampa," *Tampa Bay History*, Spring/Summer, 1987.

Page 17   The men also claimed . . . : "Two Experts Are Making Beer at New Brewery Here," *Tampa Daily Times,* December 24, 1934.

Page 18   One other brewery . . . : Kip Sharpe, "Florida Breweries in the '30s," *American Breweriana Journal,* November/December 1993.

Page 20   From Tampa Electric's trolley . . . : Robert Lehman, "Streetcars in Tampa and Saint Petersburg: A Photographic Essay," *Tampa Bay History*, Spring/Summer, 1997.

Page 23   "There were still . . .": George Carrasco, "The Florida Brewing Company," Undergraduate paper, University of South Florida, 1983.

Page 24   When the same student . . . : ibid.

Page 25   At a time when 124 brewing companies . . . : Maureen Ogle, *Ambitious Brew* (Orlando: Harcourt Books, 2006).

Page 26   Ybor City Brewing Company began . . . : Mark Albright, "Something's brewing in Ybor," *Saint Petersburg Times,* June 2, 1994.

Page 26   "Ybor City Brewing Company would enjoy a brief success . . .": Michael Canning, "Ybor brewery closes; Ybor Gold lives on," *Saint Petersburg Times,* August 15, 2003.

Page 26   The company expanded . . . : Laura Wozniak, "Summer comes to a head," *Saint Petersburg Times*, June 22, 1995.

Page 26   Perez encountered issues . . . : Cynthia Barnett, "Beer Bully," *Florida Trend*, February 1, 2001.

Chapter 2. Discount Beer, Near Beer, and Florida's Largest Craft Beer Company: Brewing in Central Florida

Page 89   The Atlantic Brewing Company began . . . : Kip Sharpe, "Florida Breweries in the 30s," *American Breweriana Journal*, November/ December 1993.

Page 90   Marlin Brewing Company only swam . . . : Steve Gordon, "Not Your Typical Florida Beauties," *Beer Cans and Brewery Collectibles*, August/September 2008.

Page 91   The lone brewery that opened . . . : John Smallshaw, "The Duncan Brewing Company, Auburndale, Florida," *American Breweriana Journal*, March–April 2006.

Page 92   Orlando waited until . . . : John Stuart, e-mail message to author on March 31, 2013.

Page 93   In June of 1992 . . . : Kirk Semple, "Do You Detect a Draft?" *Miami New Times*, May 25, 1995.

Page 93   The next mile marker . . . : Sandra Pedicini, "Shipyard brings microbrewery back to Central Florida," *Orlando Sentinel*, January 26, 2011.

Chapter 3. Local Brews after Jax Beer: Brewing in Florida's Northeast

Page 115   The city of Jacksonville's brewing . . . : *100 Years of Brewing* (Arno Press, 1903).

Page 116   Jacksonville's brewery began modestly . . . : Kip C. Sharpe "Jacksonville Brewery" (publication date and place unknown by author); article is on file at historical society.

Page 117   The whole of Jacksonville . . . : James Crooks, *Jacksonville After the Fire: 1901–1919* (Gainesville: University Press of Florida, 1991).

Page 119   "Prominent people . . .": William A. Ostner, interviewed by Kip C. Sharpe.

Page 120   Word just got out . . . : Ennis Davis, "Bootlegging and Rum-Running in Jacksonville" *MetroJacksonville.com*, October 13, 2011.

Page 124   . . . the modern six-pack . . . : many sources claim to have heard
            this rumor, but definitive proof is difficult to uncover.

Chapter 4. Beer in the Panhandle: Brewing in Florida's Northwest

Page 151   When the Naval Aeronautical . . . : Kip C. Sharpe, "The Spearman
            Brewing Company," *Pensacola Historical Society Quarterly*, summer
            1997.
Page 152   Spearman and his fellow investors . . . : Kip Sharpe, "Spearman,"
            ibid.
Page 155   If the years of World War II . . . : Kip C. Sharpe, "Spearman," ibid.

Chapter 5. Ebb and Flow of Local Beer: Brewing in South Florida

Page 174   Enter the 1930s . . . : Kip Sharpe, "Florida Breweries in the 30s,"
            American Breweriana Journal, November/December 1993.
Page 175   Around the time that Flamingo . . . : Bob Kay, "Sunshine State
            Sampler," *Beer Cans and Brewery Collectibles*, August/September
            2008.
Page 175   Miami's most infamous historical brewery . . . : Kirk Semple, "Do
            You Detect a Draft?" *Miami New Times*, May 25, 1995.
Page 176   Farther north in West Palm Beach . . . : Kip Sharpe, "in the 30s,"
            1993.
Page 179   Firehouse Brewing owner . . . : Kirk Semple, "Do You Detect a
            Draft?" *Miami New Times*, May 25, 1995.
Page 180   Durkin was quoted . . . : Cheryl Kane Heimlich, "Microbreweries
            going head-to-head," *South Florida Business Journal*, August 12,
            1996.

GLOSSARY

barrel (as measurement): A barrel is a standard measure in the brewing industry. One barrel is equivalent to 31 gallons of beer.

barrel-aged: Barrel aging is the process of taking a beer and resting it inside the wood of a barrel. That barrel usually has contained a spirit like bourbon, whiskey, or wine in its previous use, and by this process and the brewer's skill, the beer is imbued with the flavors of the last item in the barrel. An example of this would be 7venth Sun Brewery's Barrel Aged Super Fly Imperial Porter. It is also possible to age a beer in virgin wood in order to impart the flavor of the wood, as different woods have different flavors. An example of this would be Cigar City's White Oak Jai Alai IPA.

barrel brewing system: The number of a brewing system usually pertains to how much boiling wort can be generated for fermentation in one brewing session. For instance, if a brewery has a one-barrel brewing system, one barrel of beer-to-be will be produced in one brewing session and will usually be transferred into a different tank for fermentation.

dry-hopping: Dry-hopping is the addition of hops during fermentation for additional hop aroma. Dry-hopping provides additional hop character to a beer beyond the hops used in the boil.

firkin: Also called a cask. A ten-gallon container that looks like a modified keg that pours from the side. A firkin is used to make real ale—a beer that is usually separated from the rest of the fermenting wort and fermented in the firkin, sometimes with other ingredients like coffee, hops, berries, etc. for addition of new flavoring to the beer before serving.

Florida Weisse: A hybridization of the Berliner Weisse style of beer. A Berliner Weisse is a tart, low-alcohol wheat beer that is made sour and then served with a syrup to soften the tartness of the beer. A Florida Weisse takes the Berliner Weisse and instead of adding fruit syrup, the brewer infuses the beer with fruit during fermentation resulting in a fruity tartness, occasionally bordering on acidic pH, and extreme colors like purple or pink. Florida Weisses are a hybrid style indigenous to Florida and pair well with sunsets, sea breezes, palm trees, and harsh summers.

hops: The cones of the *Humulus lupulus* plant. Hops are an essential ingredient in beer and are used for flavor and aroma. Hops can be whole flower or in many instances are pelletized for easy addition to beer during boiling. Hops impart bitterness and, depending on the varietal of hop, flavors ranging from earthy grass to tropical fruit to pine sap to lemon to floral qualities to citrus flavor.

IPA: abbreviation for India Pale Ale. These beers are meant to be heavy on hop bitterness. During the period of English colonization, British beers would spoil before reaching the far-off coast of India. Brewers began adding more hops to traditional English pale ales so that the additional preservatives (and alcohol) would help the beer make the long journey unspoiled. The style then became iconic and preferred by beer drinkers, and today IPA stands as a tremendously popular style of craft beer.

treating or **treatment**: a beer is treated with fruit, spices, or another additive before serving in order to give the beer the flavor of that item. Common examples include fruit, berries, vanilla beans, coffee beans, or peppercorns.

INDEX

Mark DeNote is a traveling writer, educator, and editor who tries to keep up with the fast-paced craft beer scene in the Sunshine State.

The Great Florida Craft Beer Guide is Mark's first book. He is the editor of Florida-BeerNews.com, a website devoted to Florida craft beer, and columnist for Tampa's *Cigar City Magazine*. Mark's work has been featured in *Draft Magazine*, CraftBeer.com, and throughout the craft beer community.